Unbreakable

Unbreakable

Steve Cattell

with Lindy Greaves

Dear Liz & Matt...
Read this... don't just flog
it on ebay!

Love *Lindy Greaves*
xx

Authentic

MILTON KEYNES • COLORADO SPRINGS • HYDERABAD

Copyright © 2008 Steve Cattell and Lindy Greaves

14 13 12 11 10 09 08   7 6 5 4 3 2 1

First published 2008 by Authentic Media
9 Holdom Avenue, Bletchley, Milton Keynes, MK1 1QR, UK
1820 Jet Stream Drive, Colorado Springs, CO 80921, USA
OM Authentic Media, Medchal Road, Jeedimetla Village,
Secunderabad 500 055, A.P., India
www.authenticmedia.co.uk

Authentic Media is a division of IBS-STL U.K., limited by
guarantee, with its Registered Office at Kingstown Broadway,
Carlisle, Cumbria CA3 0HA. Registered in England & Wales No.
1216232. Registered charity 270162

British Library Cataloguing in Publication Data
A catalogue record for this book is available from the British
Library

ISBN-13: 978-1-85078-774-7

Cover Design by Phil Houghton
Print Management by Adare
Printed in Great Britain by J.H. Haynes & Co., Sparkford

Acknowledgements

I would like to thank the following people for their encouragement and assistance through the years: Richard Millington, who helped me to understand addiction to crime and to deal with it as an addiction; the former Department Chief Constable Jim Nicolson and his wife, who made me feel that I belonged and have supported my work over the years; all the prisoners trapped in the lifestyle of addiction who have listened to me; Terry Mann, chaplain of Camp Hill Prison, for his support and understanding; assistant chaplain of Brixton Prison, Chris Knight Whitcombe, for his never-ending work to help bring change; and Kingdom Faith, Horsham, for all of their hard work reaching out to youth.

I would also like to express my gratitude to several people who readers will come to know in the pages of this book. I am especially indebted to Paul, for being committed to the Truth, and to John and his wife, for inviting me to their home, for wonderful paella, for prayer and for facilitating a meeting between Paul, Lindy and myself.

This book would never have become a reality without the skill and expertise of Lindy Greaves. I'd also like to thank Charlotte Hubback, Tara Smith and Authentic Media for their support, as well as John Glass, for writing the foreword. Always, my deepest thanks and love

vi   *Acknowledgements*

go to my wife Natalie and to our children, Robbie, Terrie, Lillie and Alfie and to God, my Dad.

Foreword

My first contact with Steve was when I heard him share his story on one of the Christian television channels. I was immediately struck by his direct approach and the lack of both sentimentality in his recounting of his conversion experience or the glorification of his past.

This book recounts in necessary detail the dark journey that was travelled before he encountered Christ; but chooses to celebrate the change rather than charges that were laid against him during his criminal career.

When the woman broke the alabaster box of perfume over the feet of Jesus the pious onlookers criticised Christ on two accounts. The first was that he would allow someone with such a litany of sin anywhere near him, and the second because the act was one of such extravagance.

Jesus pointed out on that occasion that the degree of passion a persons feels when experiencing the embrace of the two arms of reconciliation – forgiveness and acceptance – is in direct proportion to the catalogue of failure to which forgiveness has been applied.

Of course passion can be a double-edged sword. On one hand Steve is passionate in his gratitude to God for bringing him into his family. On the other, Steve can exhibit an impatience with the body of Christians to which he now belongs, the Church, for not articulating the gospel as clearly as they should or accelerating the pace and passion with which they proclaim it.

When I think of Steve I think of a man who fell overboard very early in his life and has struggled his way to the surface. Now, gasping for breath in a new-found environment, he is well aware that he is saved but, like the rest of us, he knows he has still some way to swim.

There are those who exude the pristine provenance of an unsullied life but whose spiritual experience appears cold and frigid. They live like a well constructed log fire that has yet to be lit. Beautifully formed but as flame-free as they are dust-free.

The author of this book makes no pretence of ordered tidiness or religious convention. One thing that becomes immediately evident whenever you encounter him is that combustion has been applied and he lives with a desire to communicate both warmth and light.

However many criminal convictions a person may posses, it is not until we are convicted of our own sin and need for grace that change can commence. I trust that as you walk with Steve Cattell through the pages that follow you will come to discover and appreciate the power of grace that, by definition, goes beyond anything that we can expect or deserve.

John Glass, General Superintendent, Elim Pentecostal Churches

1

It's six a.m. The bathroom light is whirring and it's getting on my nerves. I finish shaving, smooth down my hair, and peer in the mirror. Do I look old? Nah, must be that damn light. I consider smashing it, but I don't want trouble with the hotel. The tiles feel cold through my socks. It's still dark outside.

I reach out to swipe the mini shampoo bottles, but then I remember the kids are too old to play 'shops' with them any more.

I put on my suit and open my briefcase. I dump the cold coffee out of my flask and make some fresh. While the kettle boils, I run through the day. We'll drive south towards the docks for our first stop, and if it goes according to plan we can be in town for the second stop before rush hour. I glance at the clock. The other two had better be ready. When the kettle finally clicks, I empty all six sachets of coffee into the flask. I throw the complimentary packet of custard creams into my case too, next to my crowbar and celluloid. I peel two hundred pounds from the wad we collected yesterday and put it in my pocket so I can pay the hotel bill when we come back, after it's all over. I pull the jewellery out of the case lining (nothing worth much – just a couple of gold chains and a brooch) and slide them under the mattress with the rest of the cash to collect later. I scan the room, set the briefcase down by the door and slip the 'Do not Disturb' sign over the doorknob. I pound on the next door down, my own special thirty-minute warning meaning 'be ready or else,' and head downstairs for some breakfast. It's going to be a long day.

After my businessman's special of two fried eggs and toast, I head back to the room for one more scan and to collect my case – and Claire and Lynn.

'Who is it?'

'Who d'you think?'

'OK, OK, Steve, give us a minute.'

'Mum's not feeling well,' Claire says as she cracks open the door.

One of the downsides of working with heroin addicts is that they're unreliable. Lynn's head appears halfway down the bathroom door. She must be on her knees in there.

'I need two minutes,' she slurs.

I sigh, put down my case and lean against the cool wallpaper. I may smoke cannabis every night, but the day I inject poison into my veins is the day they can lock me up for good and throw away the key. Claire shuts the door and I'm alone in the corridor. Sometimes silence is like darkness. I'm not sure if I like it, but it covers and calms me. There's a faint odour of disinfectant – it reminds me of something, but I can't think what. My parents' kitchen? The hospital wing at Norwich Prison?

The door bursts open and, amazingly, they're both ready to go. One of the upsides of working with heroin addicts is that they're desperate. Lynn wears sunglasses to hide her tiny pupils and CK1 masks the scent of fresh vomit. Looking at her, you wouldn't guess she was an addict. What self-respecting addict is up and functioning at seven in the morning? I always make sure we're up early and have finished our day by one p.m.

Most criminals work in the afternoon or evening. When the junkies are up and the pubs are open, the

police are out in force. You won't catch me doing anything illegal after lunch any more. Last night, when the
girls were getting off their faces on heroin – they call it
'brown' – I checked out a couple of university flats for us
to visit today. It's Easter holiday time, so most of them
should be empty.

I check the pigeonholes near the outside door to the
flats. Sometimes the postman can be really helpful.
There's mail for rooms 2, 4, 5, 6 and 7, so I try their inter-
coms. No answer. I go upstairs to let myself in.

The sound of the Yale lock clicking back brings the
first rush of adrenaline.

'Hello? Is anyone here? You know your door's open?'

Then there's the wait, that slightly sick feeling. What
if someone answers? When no one does and the door
shuts behind me, I feel a second rush. Sometimes I put
my fists together and say, 'You're mine!' like I used to
when I was a kid. Hearing my voice break the silence
makes it more real. That sensation is always like the first
time all over again. There's nothing else like knowing
that it's mine and I can take anything I want.

I do my usual gloved search. The first flat is a typical
student room. Most have at least two out of three com-
modities: computer, hi-fi, TV. I'd rather have bankbooks
and I.D. – anything Claire or Lynn can take to the bank to
withdraw cash. I don't look at the photos blue-tacked
around the mirror. I don't want to know anything about
them, other than how much money they've got in their
account or how much their stereo's worth second-hand. I
check every drawer and cupboard, but all I find amongst
the photos, letters, chewing gum and johnnies are a building society book and a ten-pound note. I pocket them,

grab a handful of CDs and leave the room as I found it, closing the door behind me. I head down to the underground car park. This is our second and last hit this morning. We'd done well on our first one, but now the girls are nearly out of heroin.

'Hey, what took you so long?' Claire whines.

Lynn is comatose on the back seat, her head lolling backwards and her mouth open, holding a square of foil in her hand. Stupid cow.

I pass Claire the book and CDs through the car window.

'Helena Jacobson will soon find she's made a rather expensive withdrawal,' I smirk. 'There's not much paperwork here and there's space in the boot, so I'm picking up CDs and electricals.'

'Fine. Get what you can and then I'll go to the bank with this one, OK? I want to get back.'

Need to, more like. Her breathing is slow, her teeth are clenched and her face is shiny with sweat, despite the cold wind.

'Alright. But you could help.'

I open the car door and wait while Claire rummages in her handbag for a plastic bag. It's painful to watch her walk. She looks more like fifty than twenty. But she's dedicated. I let myself into flat 2 while Claire's still hobbling up the stairs.

At the end of every term people load their cars with all sorts of expensive electric equipment from student flats and no one bats an eyelid. No curtains twitching, no questioning neighbours – Studentsville is thieving made easy. I fill the bag with CDs and hand it to Claire, who's hovering on the landing. They won't fetch much but I can see her calculating their worth in brown powder. I hate when she's like this, but she wouldn't be helping me if she didn't need the money, so I put up with it.

A guy in a baseball cap carrying a newspaper sack knocks on the outside door. I let him in. He looks fed up as he drops a paper outside each door.

'Alright, mate?' I raise my eyebrows. 'End of term again, eh?'

What poor sod would want to do that all day for peanuts? He nods at us. He obviously doesn't want to chat. I go back in for a newish Sony hi-fi I'd spotted, a small one that will fit in the boot with the TVs. It could be worth a couple of hundred second-hand. When I come out of the flat again the delivery guy's gone. Claire hugs the plastic bag to her chest. She's sweating profusely, covered in goose bumps and shaking. We need to get to the bank fast. If she isn't in any shape to defraud banks and building societies she's no use at all. It's turning into a bad morning.

'Ready?' I ask her. She nods and begins staggering down the stairs. The hi-fi cord is trailing and the plug whacks me on the back of the leg at every step. I've got grit in my eye, but I can't do anything about it because my hands are full. I'm tired and I need my coffee and my money from the bank. Claire stops suddenly and I almost knock her flying.

'Police! Police! Stay where you are. This is the police.'

Instinctively Claire flicks her heroin out of her pocket and steps on it.

'Keep your hands where we can see them.'

I know the score – being arrested is as much a part of my life as burgling houses. I put the hi-fi down slowly, keeping my hands visible. I show them my empty palms as I straighten up. I didn't see any guns, but it's better to be safe. If you do anything stupid when you're in front of a nervous copper with a gun in his hand, you might as well jump off a bridge. One of them takes the car keys out of my pocket while his mate snaps my hands into cuffs behind my back. They're too tight. I'll have marks on my wrists by the time I get to the station.

'Steve Cattell, I'm arresting you on suspicion of burglary. You do not have to say anything but it may harm your defence if you do not mention when questioned something which you later rely on in court. Anything you do or say may be given in evidence.'

I come easy – not like Claire. A minute ago she seemed ready to drop, but now her lipsticked mouth opens and a torrent of foul words spews out as she struggles against the officer's grip. It's a bizarre sight, this woman in a suit thrashing around like an animal. Her hair and eyes are wild and she snorts as she tries to break free. The officer yelps when she bites him on the arm. Another policeman rushes over to restrain her. The first one looks embarrassed.

Lynn's still asleep in the car, or at least she's pretending she is. Another officer, a woman, is standing with her hand on the car window.

'Stay calm, please,' she says to Lynn. As if comatose weren't the height of calm. 'I'm going to open the door now, don't make any sudden movements.'

Turns out they'd been following us all morning in three unmarked cars. That newspaper guy I'd felt sorry for was undercover. They couldn't do me for burglary unless they could prove I was actually entering the individual flats – otherwise it would have just been attempted burglary. I guess it was about time. I'd been working Portsmouth for nearly five years and done about three or four thousand burglaries. Their commander must have been giving the burglary squad a hard time because of me.

The heavy yellow door slams behind me and I check out my new home. Citric yellow paint's been daubed over the dents kicked into the bottom of the door by hundreds of boots. The walls are half yellow, half grimy white – probably a shrink warned the interior decorator that painting a cell all one colour might drive us mad. Someone's clothes are folded on the bottom bunk. I toss my tobacco and cigarette paper onto the top bunk. There are no magazines or photos, no sign of what my cellmate is like. It's an anonymous cell – I've never been here before but it feels familiar.

I haul myself onto the bed. It's not long enough for me to lie down stretched out and the white sheets scrape the back of my neck. There's a television in the corner, like the one in the boot of my car – or wherever it is now – but I can't be bothered to get down to turn it on. There are little indents on the ceiling where the keepsakes of previous inmates have been stuck and then removed, pulling the plaster off. I rate the bed as prison-typical – bearable if you lie on your back, but if you lie on your side too long the springs dig into your hipbone. I hate the top bunk. I contemplate kicking off to get me into solitary – no top bunk, no cellmate.

There'd been no point pleading 'Not guilty.' There I was, inside a flat carrying stolen goods, the building society book in the car and the cash and jewellery at the hotel. I'd confessed in the interview. In less than twenty-four hours I'd been cuffed; driven to the station; searched; relieved of keys, mobile and celluloid; read my rights; held in a cell; questioned; charged. I'd posed for a mug shot, had my fingertips scanned and cheeks swabbed. I'd been denied bail, driven to prison, searched again, interviewed and here I am. Remand.

Then there was my phone call. Natalie didn't even sound angry or surprised. I guess we've had this conversation before.

'Nat?'

'What's happened?'

'Look, Nat . . .'

'I knew something was wrong. You're in prison, aren't you?'

'Yeah. I've been denied bail.'

'How long this time?'

'I dunno. Could be three years once I get to court.'

'Right.'

'You and the kids'll be alright.'

'Yes.'

'Speak to you next week maybe?'

'OK.'

'OK.'

'Look Steve, I've got to go. Sorry.'

'Yeah me too, say night to the kids for me.'

'Bye Steve.'

I held the phone for a minute. I didn't even use up the time I was allowed.

Well, that was that. Was the tough act for me, herself or the kids? What if she left me? I probably wouldn't stop her. I remember the last time I saw her – she was sleeping, her eyelids flickering. She looked small in the bed on her own – like a child. I never wake her when I leave. Now I'm here and she's home. Or am I home too? I close my eyes and wait to meet my cellmate.

2

I was born 14th May 1957 in North London. My sister left home before I was born and I rarely saw her. My three brothers were much older, too, and they couldn't be bothered with me.

'Can I play football with you today? Please?' I stood in the kitchen waiting for them.

'Forget it. It's football, not babysitting.'

Mum looked up from her ironing, silently begging them to say yes.

'He's too small, Mum. He'll get hurt and cry.'

They ran out laughing. Mum shook her head and went back to her ironing. 'You're under my feet, Steve, go out and play.'

My dad worked nights as a postman and slept during the day. If I was too loud, he'd wake up and thump me. So I spent a lot of time playing, and fighting, in the street. I visited the sweetshop on the corner most days. Sometimes I'd take money from my mum's purse, other times from my dad's pockets. My dad slept with his trousers under his pillow. He didn't trust anyone. While he slept, I'd creep in, hide under the bed and wait, really quietly. I knew the first thing he'd do when he woke up was get up to go to the toilet. As soon as he left the room I'd reach up and grab money out of his trouser pocket. Soon I realised I didn't have to steal money to buy sweets – I could just steal the sweets. I don't know why I did it.

I saw other kids shoplifting, but certainly not every boy who pinches sweets from a sweetshop ends up spending twenty-four years of his life behind bars.

My parents were always arguing – and it was always about me. When I got into trouble, which was often, my mum stuck up for me. My dad never did. The most I could hope for was that my dad wouldn't be home when I got caught.

'Let me go! You're choking me!'

'Be quiet, boy,' old Mr Elliott ordered as he dragged me home.

I knew the look on Mum's face as soon as she opened the door.

'Mrs Cattell?'

'Yes? What has he done now?'

'I'm afraid I will have to call the police if I find him in the street throwing stones at our window again.'

'Yes, thank you, I understand. I'll take care of it.' She closed the door and shook her head.

'Is Dad home? Are you going to tell him?'

'No. Not this time. Please try to stay out of trouble, Steve. Please.'

'I will, Mum. I promise. Can I go out and play now?'

'No you can't. You need to stay inside with me for a while.'

'Aw, please? There's nothing to do here. When can I go out again?'

'After lunch,' she sighed. 'But if this happens again . . .'

'It won't.'

We both knew it probably would.

I laid on my bed until lunch and stared at the ceiling. That was a close one. If Dad had been home, I'd have been beaten for sure.

School was even worse. When I was there, I was usually fighting with other kids or with the teachers. One day Mr Richards walloped me for something I hadn't done. It was so unfair, I hit him back and got expelled. Other parents didn't want their children playing with me. I was a bad kid. I spent most of my time on my own. I started taking my dad's cigarettes as well as his money. After a few attempts, I could smoke a whole cigarette properly without coughing or feeling sick. So I started smoking them whenever I could get my hands on them. I was seven.

I started at another school, and it was the same story. I got into trouble without even trying.

'Hey, new kid, give us your sandwiches.' I looked up from my lunch to see two big boys with shaved heads standing over me.

'You can have them. I'm not really hungry.'

They pushed me around a bit, but I wouldn't bite. When the bell rang for afternoon lessons, one of the boys in my class came up to me. He was fair-haired, fair-skinned and wiry, with the same shaven head.

'Hi, my name's Gary. Those boys are the best fighters in the school, so you better be careful.'

'OK, thanks.'

'They used to pick on me, but now you're the new boy. How old are you?'

'Eight.'

'Me too. But you're tall. You look older.'

The bullies hassled me every day. I tried to ignore it. I knew if I was expelled from this school, the beating I'd get from my dad would be much worse than the last one. So I kept my head down, hoping they'd get bored and start picking on someone else. But every day for weeks, it was two of them against one of me. One lunchtime, while they had me pinned into the usual corner of the playground, something in me snapped. I was out of control – punching, kicking, biting.

I smashed the two of them to pieces with all the other kids looking on. It felt good, watching them on the floor with their hands over their heads. Seeing them cry. Hearing them beg me to stop. Watching them shuffle off together.

For half an hour I was a hero: the other kids even lifted me on their shoulders and took me on a lap of the playground. It was the best feeling ever. They didn't do it because I'd won and had taken over as the best fighter in the school, and they didn't do it because they wanted to be my friends. They did it because I gave two bullies what they deserved. No one likes a bully. And I wasn't a bully.

My victory didn't make me more popular, though. If anything it made me lonelier. Because of the reputation I earned that day, bullies left me alone. But everyone else left me alone too – everyone except Gary.

Gary was my first friend. Although we met at school, we didn't spend much time there. He lived four streets away from me so we saw each other every day. If we weren't suspended anyway we'd bunk off school, get into fights, smoke. Neither of us got on with our families and we were always in trouble. Other children weren't allowed to play with us because of our behaviour. But that made our friendship stronger. We were misfits, but we were misfits together. He was my brother and the North London streets were our playground. We'd always back each other up, no matter how big the other boys we were fighting were. We understood each other. Some weekends he'd steal a fiver from his mum's purse and we'd go on the train to the fun fair at Southend. When the money ran out, we'd lift a purse from a lady's handbag or a wallet out of someone's back pocket. Part of the sport was running along the beach being chased by an angry man we'd robbed. One time a man in a suit chased us all the way to the station. The train was just leaving as we jumped on. As the train gathered speed, we waved and pulled faces to the suit who was standing red-faced and panting on the platform. We laughed about that all the way home. I was more at home with Gary than I was in the four walls of my house.

The first time the police came looking for me, I was eight years old. There was a rapping on the door in the middle of the night. I heard the grunt as my dad got out of bed, the creaking of the stairs, the front door scraping open. All the while my dad was fuming and swearing about what time it was. Then all I could make out were muffled voices.

Finally I heard a bellow up the stairs. 'Steven! Get down here now – the police are here.'

I hurried down the stairs in my pyjamas, jumping the last four steps. The officers looked huge standing in the doorway. Even in the gloom I could see how shiny their shoes were. I didn't know why they were there. They asked me questions about Gary.

'When did you last see him?'

'Yesterday afternoon.'

'Did you see him tonight?'

'No, sir.'

'Were you with him at all this evening?'

'No, sir.' Should I say yes? Hadn't I just answered the same question twice?

The police said that was all they needed to know.

After they left, my dad ordered me back to bed. 'And don't let me ever be woken up at two o'clock in the morning by the police again, do you hear me? If I find out you were lying to the police, boy, your life won't be worth living . . .'

I ran back upstairs, my mind racing. What had Gary done? We'd been stealing apples from a garden in his street that afternoon, but surely the police wouldn't be interested in that. Would they?

I didn't hear what happened until the next day. Gary had gone to the Islington power station with a fifteen-year-old boy who had sent him over the roof to the night watchman's hut to steal a packet of cigarettes. Our cigarettes often came from such sources. As Gary crawled across, the asbestos roof gave way beneath him. He fell into the power station between the two conductors. Half of Islington had a power cut for about two hours while the energy flowed through Gary's body. He was pulled out naked: his clothes had been burned off. His skin was charred black. He died in hospital in the early hours of that morning.

My mum said that she was sorry and that she knew how I felt. But she had no idea. I didn't even know how I felt. I had one friend and now he was gone. I was hurt. I was angry with Gary for dying and leaving me behind Every morning I woke up and I was alone. No one else wanted to be my friend and I didn't want anyone else to be my friend.

Nobody ever mentioned Gary to me again. I overheard my parents talking in the kitchen one night when I snuck in from having a smoke.

'. . . sad, but that boy was nothing but trouble.'

'He was a bad influence . . .'

I walked in and they stopped talking.

After being expelled from a third school, I was diagnosed with behavioural difficulties and taken to see a child psychologist. The first session went something like this:

'Steve, can you tell me why you play truant from school?'

'I don't know.'

'Why do you think you get into fights?'

'I don't know.'

'I see. Steve, who are your friends?'

'I don't have any friends.'

'OK, can you tell me about that? Why do you think it is that you don't have any friends?'

'I don't know.'

The second session wasn't much better. Towards the end of the hour he started asking me about my parents. I had nothing to say about them, either.

'Do you think,' the psychologist finally asked me, 'that perhaps your problems and behaviour could be a result of your parents not being your real parents?'

Not my real parents? I'd succeeded in acting as bored as I felt for nearly two hours with this man. But he had me here.

'What?'

'I was wondering if the fact that your grandparents have acted as your parents has caused difficulties for you?'

'What are you talking about?' Grandparents? How could they be my grandparents? If Mum and Dad were my grandparents, who were my parents? He was talking a load of rubbish.

He left the room to talk to my mother in the waiting room.

She walked me home without a word. When we got home, I wanted to go out. She made me sit down while she boiled the kettle.

'Steve, I know this is going to be hard for you to understand,' she began. And she told me that my big sister was actually my mother. Which made the people I'd been calling Mum and Dad my grandparents, and the brothers who didn't want anything to do with me my uncles.

'Can I still call you Mum? And Dad?'

'Of course you can.' My mother, who was really my grandmother, tried to smile.

I went out for a smoke. I'd never known anyone who was adopted. Now at least I knew why I didn't fit in. They wouldn't have chosen me if they had a choice, which they didn't.

I kicked the wall by the bus stop and stubbed my toe. Some kids drove by and yelled insults at me. I felt hot anger surge through me. I never trusted anyone from that day forward. I hated that I'd been lied to. I hated that my family, neighbours, the psychologist all knew about it when I didn't.

Years later I was told that my mother was raped when she was fourteen and I was the result. Who knows if that's the truth or not? A pregnant fourteen-year-old might say anything because she's scared. I'll never know.

Instead of going to school the next day, I tried something new. I broke into someone's house. The back door was unlocked – all I had to do was unlatch the gate to the garden and open the door. I wandered around the house, looking at their stuff. There was a family picture on the mantelpiece, one of those holiday pictures with everyone smiling. I bet these are their real parents, I thought as I swallowed hard. The clock next to the picture looked like it might be expensive, so I took it and left. I didn't care if anyone saw me, and I didn't particularly care what I stole. I burgled seven houses on my street that week. People weren't as security-conscious then, so even if doors were locked I could usually find an open window to clamber through.

All of those seven houses belonged to the people on the street who had been nice to me – one lady had knitted me a jumper each Christmas, another had bought me an ice cream and someone else had taken me to the football. I targeted them on purpose because I believed they knew why I didn't belong and what I was – they'd taken pity on me and I hated them for it.

Climbing through one window into a yellow-tiled kitchen brought back memories of the day, two or three years before, when I'd fallen off a wall outside this house and grazed my arm. The lady had rushed out, scooped me up, and carried me inside. She'd sat me in this kitchen and made me a cup of sweet tea. I had sipped it, trying not to cry while she gently dabbed at my grazes with wet cotton wool. I remember wishing my mum was more like her. Except it wasn't my mum, it was my grandmother, pretending. And that lady who was so nice to me probably only did it because she knew.

I looked around the kitchen. There were some tins along the wall next to the cooker. I dumped them all out looking for cash. I didn't find any, but I left the yellow-tiled floor covered with sugar and tea leaves. I opened all the kitchen drawers but found only cutlery and cooking utensils. An old-fashioned writing desk in the lounge had a locked drawer. I searched in vain for a key and then grabbed a kitchen knife from one of the drawers. It felt good in my hand. Back in the lounge, I slid the knife into the gap where the drawer joined the writing desk. Moving it right to left, I heard a click. The catch had flicked back. It was a satisfying feeling – somehow more satisfying than seeing the two five-pound notes as I slid the drawer open. I stuffed them in my pocket and returned to the kitchen. I was about to replace the knife where I'd found it but changed my mind. I clamped it

between my teeth, like a pirate, as I scrambled back
through the window and made my escape.

I started using that knife to flick back the catches on
windows. It was my first tool and I carried it with me
wherever I went. With that knife, I could do anything.

Within a week the police were at my door for the second time. They took me down to the station this time. I
had to have an adult with me. I looked at the people
who used to be my parents: Mum was sobbing and I
knew from the look on Dad's face that I'd be getting a
beating when I got home. Only a few weeks ago I would
have wanted my mum there with me, but I was so angry
with them I didn't care any more. They both came – I
don't think my mum trusted my dad to go with me on
his own. I didn't even care that I'd been caught. I think I
almost expected to be. I didn't do it because I wanted to
get away with robbery – I did it because I was angry. The
policemen asked me questions. I didn't say much. I
didn't have to – it was clear I was guilty. Eventually I
was cautioned for seven burglaries.

'Will I go to prison?' I asked the police officer.

'Not this time, son. But you keep going the way
you're going and it won't be long.'

3

The most important thing I learned from that interview
with the police was that I couldn't be charged for anything until I was ten years old. Until I was ten, I was
untouchable. That knowledge was a licence to steal. I
knew that whatever I took, whatever house I broke into,
I would just be arrested and taken back home.

I discovered I loved taking things that weren't mine.
Every time I went anywhere, I stole – money, alarm
clocks, radios – it didn't matter what it was. I sold the
goods to second-hand shops, telling the owners that my
dad had asked me to sell the things for him or that my
uncle had died and left them to me in his will. I realise
now that they probably knew they were nicked but
could make a better profit if they bought gear cheaply
from me.

Soon I couldn't go a week without burgling a house. I
enjoyed the thieving as much as spending the proceeds.
I was always caught, but it didn't matter. I was nine. I'd
burgle, be arrested, cautioned, released, burgle again. It
was like a game – and it was much more exciting than
the games other kids my age were playing.

I also started running away from home on a regular
basis. I slept on the stairs of blocks of flats, in graveyards, in tree houses, in people's garden sheds.
Sometimes if I was hungry, I'd wait until it was dark and
crawl through a window into someone's kitchen and

steal food. It was a vicious cycle, though. The more I
stayed away from home, the worse home was when I
was there. Mum and Dad fought more and more. Mum
still stuck up for me every time the police brought me
home. Dad beat the life out of me with a stick. He never
beat my older brothers, who I still couldn't think of as
my uncles. Each time the stick came crashing down, I
became a bit stronger and a lot angrier.

As the winter cold set in, though, I had no choice but
to spend more time at home. I could sleep at home and
put up with it or freeze to death. One day as I turned
onto my street, I saw a policeman leaving my house. I
crouched behind a wall and watched him cross the road
to his car, take off his hat and get in. When the car was
out of sight I walked gingerly towards my house. I could
hear the fight before I got there – my mum's pleading
voice and my dad shouting and stamping. I stopped at
the door to listen.

'Didn't I tell you we should never have kept the bas-
tard to start with?'

I felt sick. I ran. Nowhere. Anywhere. I didn't care. I
tried not to think about what I'd heard. But I couldn't
think of anything else. That first night I found a shed to
sleep in a few streets away. I pulled a tarpaulin over my
head to try to keep out the cold. The smell of mould and
soil made me want to retch, but when I put my head out,
the icy wind rushed in through the broken window and
around the door and cut into my cheeks and ears. Were
they worrying about me? No – I'd heard what he'd said.
I knew what I was. They never wanted me, and I was
never going back there. I lay awake shivering most of
the night. The next day I ate a couple of apples from the
tree in the garden and a packet of crisps I took from a
newsagent. I dreaded another freezing night under that
stinking tarpaulin, but I didn't have a choice – I couldn't

go home. The second night was worse than the first. Every time I replayed those words in my head I felt a fresh wave of hatred towards him – towards them, but the cold was numbing my resolve. I was going to freeze to death. So towards the end of that second night, when I knew he'd still be at work, I returned.

I wasn't sure what she would say. I stood on the doorstep in the dark and told myself I didn't care. But when Mum opened the door in her dressing gown and saw me, some of the lines around her eyes and across her forehead softened, and I knew she'd been worried. She sent me up to bed with a mug of hot cocoa. I'd barely drained the cup when Dad arrived home. He usually went straight to bed when he got in from his night shift. I sat in bed and waited, glaring at the door. I heard his footsteps on the stairs. The landing light was on and I could see shadows under the door.

'Come out here,' he growled.

I didn't move. The door swung open and he stood grimacing, stick in hand. I stayed where I was. Slowly he walked over to me and towered above me. He raised the stick. I shot out of the bed towards the door but he was too quick. He grabbed hold of my arm as I reached the landing. I spun round.

'Get off me.' The words I'd said a thousand times in my head sounded strange coming out of my mouth. Anger had finally conquered fear.

He paused for a moment, stunned.

'Who the hell . . .' He raised the stick again in fury. As it struck me, I kicked him as hard as I could. Although he was a lot heavier than me he was off-balance, and he staggered backwards towards the stairs. Time stood still as I watched him fall all the way to the bottom. For a few seconds he didn't move. Then his eyes opened and he looked up at me.

'If you touch me again, I'll smash your head in,' I said and went back to bed.

A few weeks later, I reached the crucial age of ten and everything changed. The next time I was arrested I went to juvenile court and a care order was placed on me. I think after my dad fell down the stairs, my mum wasn't about to fight to keep me. Social Services sent me to an assessment centre called Stamford House and then placed me in a house with dormitories. I ran away the first night I was there. I was classified as 'vulnerable' because of my age so, whenever I ran away, the police were always called. I usually managed to elude them by heading back to the area I came from – passing lots of police cars looking for me along the way. At night I slept on stairs or in graveyards. During the day I stole food, or money to buy it. The police always caught up with me eventually, sometimes after a chase, and sent me back to Stamford House.

The third time I ran away from the assessment centre, I went with Carly. She was about a year older than me. I didn't fancy her or anything like that. We just got on well. We shared a hatred for authority and a passion for burglary. Carly introduced me to sleeping on the roofs of laundry buildings.

'Here, come sit over here beside the vents,' she called.

'No thanks, here's fine. Great campsite,' I muttered. 'Must be the coldest place in the country tonight.' The wind was fierce and I was tired. First the close shave with the guard at the centre, then the climb up here.

'Come on, Steve, it's warm. I've done it loads of times.'

I bit my pride with my chattering teeth and ventured over. It was warm. I sat down and hugged my knees to my chest.

'And look,' Carly said, peering down over the edge of the roof. 'You can see for miles. If the police are here they won't see us, but we can see them.'

'That's pretty cool,' I admitted.

We had a decent night's sleep that night, and for three nights after that, until the police finally caught up with us. I was returned to the assessment centre and Carly was taken somewhere else.

I ran away a few more times on my own until I was finally placed in the secure unit at Stamford House. This small unit consisted of cells with bars on the window. The bed was concrete. There was a fireproof mattress and a proper cell door. I was to stay there for at least two years. We exercised in a small yard with a net on the roof to prevent us from standing on each other's shoulders and climbing over the wall. The food was all right, and when we were allowed out of our cells, we could play table tennis or sit on the big comfy chairs to watch television – and then I could smoke a sneaky fag or nick some food from the kitchens. There was an education room, but anyone who refused education was locked in their cell. Most of the time I was locked in my cell, sometimes twenty-three hours a day. Once I spent an entire week in there. I kicked away at the inside steel door, but there was a wooden door on the outside so no one could hear all the kicking and screaming. I shouted obscenities at the staff. I was angry. I hated the world. I didn't understand why I was there. I cried. I don't know what it was I craved. A psychologist might suggest I needed love, but I didn't know what that was. Whatever it was, it wasn't to be found at Stamford House.

Every evening when I went to bed, my chest hurt. My heart beat so fast it felt like it was going to explode. I didn't know what was happening. I couldn't catch my breath and thought I was going to die. I jumped out of bed and walked up and down the cell. My mouth was so dry I couldn't swallow. I tried to yawn, anything to get my breath back. Gradually I stopped shivering and felt calmer. When I got back into bed it started again. This happened every night. Many years later, doctors diagnosed this hyperactive disorder that still affects me. I continue to struggle to get to sleep without medication. But then I didn't tell anybody about it. Every night I was terrified that I might stop breathing in my sleep and die.

The more time I spent alone in my cell, the more I began to hate the outside world and everything in it. When I thought about being released, all I wanted to do was punish and destroy everyone and everything on the outside. I tried to smash everything in my cell – a futile mission when most things were made of concrete, although I did injure some of the warders. Sometimes I flew into rages and kicked and hit and bit anyone who tried to restrain me. They gave me sedatives to control my behaviour. They were really hard to swallow and I hated the way they made me feel, but I didn't have a choice. My bedtime ritual was a tranquilliser then a wine gum, tranquilliser, wine gum. By the time morning came everything was so hazy, I could barely remember my name.

I didn't mind the other kids in the secure unit. I made a lot of friends there that I met up with later in life on the street, in other prisons, and borstals. After my two years in the secure unit was up, I was assessed for an approved school that was run by Brothers from some kind of monastery. They walked around in robes and forced us to go to church. I ran away the first night and was brought back very quickly the next day and beaten with a stick. After that I was made to stand in the middle of the yard. The winter rain was icy on my bare legs. I stood there in a pair of shorts for nearly four hours.

Then they gave me two left plimsolls without laces to wear and took my clothes away from me every night so that I couldn't abscond. That just made me more determined. One night I got as far as Dartford Station in just a pair of pyjamas – no socks or shoes. I made it back to London and dressed myself with clothes from washing lines in people's gardens. I was caught and taken back to the approved school. I escaped over and over again – and each time I was beaten.

The Brothers gave us very little food. Every night after we'd been told to keep quiet, the dormitory was filled with the miserable grumbles of empty bellies. Some nights I levered myself through the dormitory window, climbed across the roofs and into the pantry. I'd share out the food I stole with the other boys. That way I knew they wouldn't grass me up. There was a shop across the road that we were allowed to visit. I also stole from there and brought the food back to eat at night in the dormitory.

Some nights the Brothers who ran the school came into the dormitory and told one of the smaller, quieter boys to wait outside. We never knew exactly what went on, but we had a pretty good idea. The boys that were picked were the sorts of boys who wouldn't say anything. I was safe: boys who were likely to fight back were left alone. Not long ago some of these Brothers were charged for offences against the boys in their care.

One more escape, and the approved school didn't want me back any more. I was sent to a children's home where I met up again with Carly. She'd spent the years since we last saw each other in and out of different children's homes. It was so easy to run away from the children's homes. We escaped most weeks. After a few months, I was placed back in the secure unit at Stamford House for assessment. I didn't know what happened to

Carly. After another year at Stamford House, Social Services took me into care. I was released to a foster family when I was thirteen.

My middle-class foster parents both worked in a school. He was a maths teacher. They were short-term foster carers. Each child they took in stayed for three to six months, then another one came. They told me that the girl who stayed in my room before me was called Carly. Could it have been the same Carly I met in Stamford House? I asked a lot of questions about her. It had been over a year since I saw her – when we were in the children's home together. Apparently she hadn't wanted to leave the foster home. She had got on really well with the foster parents and their two young children and felt settled there and part of the family. But once her six months was up, she had to go. A week later Carly was found dead – she'd put her head in an oven and gassed herself.

Gradually I started to relax into a family lifestyle. My foster parents had more time for me than the adults in the children's homes and the secure unit ever had. I'd been there four months when I saw one of the cheques they received from Social Services. It seemed like an obscene amount of money to me. I realised that these people weren't looking after me because they loved or cared about me – I was a financial arrangement, paying the mortgage on their house. I was gutted. I burgled their house and ran away. Crime was the only way I knew to lash out at the people and the systems I hated so much.

When the police caught up with me again they placed me in another children's home. It wasn't long before I was back into the cycle – running away, burgling houses, fighting, getting arrested and dragged back – and soon the children's home returned me to Social Services.

I spent most days in my social worker's office while she phoned every single children's home to try to find me a placement. At the end of each day, when she still hadn't found me a placement, she drove me to a bed and breakfast at Finsbury Park. She'd check the room was suitable and leave me there for the night. The next morning I went back to the office to go through the same routine. Nobody wanted me, so I stayed in the B & B. I was given £1.50 every day for food – more than enough for a thirteen-year-old boy to eat, but it lasted five minutes in the sweet shop and I starved the rest of the day unless I stole food – which I usually did.

I'd long ago discarded the kitchen knife and carried a smaller blade instead for flicking back catches on windows and doors. The knife worked a charm on the B & B owner's bedroom door. He obviously didn't have a bank account – I'd never seen so much money in my life. I came out of that room with about seven and a half thousand pounds. In those days houses cost six thousand pounds. I was thirteen years old and I couldn't quite believe my luck. I could go where I wanted, eat what I wanted, do what I wanted – I didn't have to answer to anybody. I was free. Suddenly the power of money thrilled me as much as the crime itself.

4

It came as no great surprise to me – or to anyone else, I suppose – that I was arrested for burglary a few days later. This time, though, I was taken to juvenile court and sentenced to three months in a detention centre. After nearly two years in the secure unit, how bad could it be? I soon found out. There were no comfy chairs or televisions here, just a long list of rules. For example: up at six every morning – no excuses. Call everyone 'sir.' Don't walk – march. Complete the daily fitness regime – or else (those who passed out had a bucket of water thrown over them and were made to finish regardless). No talking unless given permission. We were required to stand in our underwear in the parade ground in the middle of winter. Punishments included scrubbing floors with toothbrushes while the officers watched and smirked. All of this fed my anger and hate. And all the physical fitness training just made me stronger and faster and harder for the police to catch.

I had only been released for a couple of months when I was arrested for burglary again. The cycle was the same as it had been when I was nine, except that I was given custodial sentences. I burgled and was arrested, charged, imprisoned, released; then I burgled again. I didn't live anywhere longer than three months. Because I was only thirteen, they couldn't lock me up for long. And it never took me long to burgle again after my release. It was a vicious cycle, but it was the only one I knew.

But then, one day, the arrest didn't go quite as expected. Instead of going to a detention centre, I was shoved into a prison van en route to Ashford Remand Centre to await sentencing. I'd never been to a prison before. The sweatbox I was locked in was just over a metre wide and so low I couldn't stand up. Although I was small enough to sit, I couldn't – I smelled all the people who'd been locked in here before me. It was just as well I couldn't see what was on the floor. I bent my neck to get a better view out the grimy window. We passed a couple of houses that looked promising. I looked for a landmark – at the end of the road was a pub called 'The Swan.' I'd remember where they were so I could burgle them on the way back home after my release.

And then we were there – home sweet home until my sentencing. I shifted my weight to the other side of the sweatbox and made out the enormous gates as we passed through, and the blackened bricks of the prison wall beyond. The van stopped and they let us out. High above, coils of razor glinted in the sun. The coils running along near the cell windows wore limp bits of clothing and bed sheets. The ground under the cell windows was littered with more clothes; apple cores; crisp packets; rotting, rejected prison food – apparently those tiny windows served as garbage chutes for all the things the prisoners didn't want in their cells. The stench made me gag.

We were jostled inside and a screw gave each of us a rub down search after we handed over our belongings. One of the screws unlocked a big iron gate and shoved us into a room with benches along the walls. If it weren't for the thick iron bars on the window, we could have been in a sports changing room.

'Wait here,' the screw barked as he turned the key. As if we had a choice. 'If you need the toilet, knock.' He pointed to three toilets directly opposite the room. We could hear and smell everything, and one didn't even have a door. I decided I could wait.

After about an hour that seemed like ten, the screw took us to the showers.

'Hand over your clothes,' they commanded as we filed past. I figured it was so they could check the pockets and linings for drugs. But then they gave us uniforms – I'd never had to wear a uniform before. It was uncomfortable and the trousers were too short. I didn't have the will or the right to complain but stumbled into the exercise yard behind everyone else.

'Right. Under fifteens here,' a screw ordered. 'Be quiet and stay in this line. When everyone gets their uniform we'll march to the juvenile block.' Ashford was an adult prison but there was a detached block for juveniles. I was still thirteen.

Once we were all outside – there were about twelve of us – we were shuffled into threes and marched over to the block. The uniform scraped my skin. I was hungry and tired and I could tell the officers were making us march because they were on a power trip. So when it was my group's turn to go, I spoke to the screw that was giving the orders.

'I'm on remand. I haven't been sentenced. I haven't been found guilty of the crime I've been accused of, so I shouldn't have to follow the rules and march until I'm actually convicted.'

He exchanged glances with the other screws. I tensed – ready for a physical punishment – but then he turned to me and almost smiled.

'Name?' he demanded.

'Cattell. Steve Cattell.'

He looked at his clipboard. 'Fine. Walk over,' he said.

I walked over to the block. All the other boys were locked into cells. As I stood waiting my turn I saw them out of the corner of my eye first. Four prison officers approached, taking their truncheons out of their belts as they came upon me. There was nowhere to run. It was too late. The first whack knocked me to the floor. I yelped as the blows stung my arms and back. I tried to get into a ball with my hands over my head while they kicked me again and again. I saw blood on the floor and knew it was mine. I tried to roll away, but one of them grabbed hold of my testicles and another grabbed hold of my hair and they dragged me, screaming in pain and terror, over to the punishment block more than a five-minute walk away – upstairs, downstairs, along landings – I was dragged the whole way. The uniform tore and burned grazes into my skin. They threw me, covered in blood, into the punishment cell. I crawled into the corner and shivered. I was just in my underwear – most of the uniform had been ripped off me during the assault. They continued to kick and punch me while I begged for them to stop. I realised that they were getting more pleasure from my crying and pleading than from the violence itself.

The next morning I stood in front of the governor. I had refused to put clothes on and I faced him covered in bruises and dry matted blood. All night I'd rehearsed what I was going to say to him. Even if he didn't believe what I said, he couldn't ignore my injuries – those screws were not going to get away with what they'd done.

'Your officers,' I began, 'beat me with their truncheons–'

'I know what happened.' He cut me off and held up his hand. 'We cannot be held responsible for what happens to prisoners when we restrain them during escape attempts.'

'But–' I blurted out in my shock.

'But nothing, boy. If you try to escape again, it will be even worse. I'm warning you now.'

'They beat me!' I was nearly in tears.

'Nonsense. My officers wouldn't beat anyone. That is a false accusation, and if you continue to make false accusations, you will get into deeper trouble.'

'It's not fair, they –'

'A word of advice, boy. Keep your head down. Do as you're told. Don't talk back.'

Anger and disbelief surged through me in waves. I thought I might throw up.

Back in my cell I promised myself that I would never scream out to anybody in authority ever again. I would never cry. I would never show fear. I would never suffer pain. No matter what they did. If they broke my arm I'd put my other arm out and fight with that until that was broken too. And I would never give in. If they gave me seven days in the punishment block, I would ask for fourteen. And if they opened the door after fourteen, I'd kick the door shut and stay down there for twenty-eight. I would not let them beat me.

Ever.

Having a sentence, knowing how long I'd have to hang on, was easy. Waiting for a court date, not knowing how long I'd be there – that was hard. But my hatred for authority got me through. Everything fed it. I clung to it. Becoming unbreakable was my all-consuming focus. I smashed my hands into the cell walls as hard as I could. Every time I had a cup of tea, I plunged my hand into the scalding liquid – first for five seconds, the next time for ten, then fifteen, until I couldn't feel the burning. Never cry out. Never give in.

Hate everyone. If no one could break me, no one could hurt me.

I reacted violently to bullies so they left me alone and moved on to more vulnerable teenagers. I was building a reputation within the prison system that began to follow me around. People saw me in fights, saw that I could handle myself and refused to be beaten, and they told other people. He's a nutter. Leave him alone. So eventually I didn't have to fight any more. I served more than twenty different sentences in Ashford and other institutions like it during my juvenile years. I was beaten again, and worse, but not once did I cry out. Not once did I let them win.

I'd served three days of my second stint at the detention centre when two big guys came into my cell. It wasn't lock down and my cellmate had gone down to the TV room. It was one of the few times I could be in the cell on my own. Although I'd been locked in there all night, I was enjoying my own space, lying on the top bunk listening to my Walkman. It was plugged into a PP9 battery, the battery of choice for prisoners because they lasted for two or three months. Although the battery was big and heavy, like a brick, that wasn't a problem for someone who spends most of his day in a cell. Portability isn't an issue.

I continued listening to my music as these guys bumbled in. One stank of sour sweat, which I couldn't understand because our shower day had been the day before, and the other had a red-raw face from a shaving rash. The bed was behind the half-open door and they didn't see me right away. They walked over to the table under the window. The sweaty one picked up my packet of tobacco and put it in his pocket. When they turned and saw me watching them they looked surprised, but when they realised I was younger and on my own they smirked and walked towards the door.

'What do you think you're doing?' I couldn't help myself.

'Shut up!' the stale-smelling guy sneered. He came right over to the bed, yanked out my earphones and put his face right in mine.

'And you know what else?' he continued. 'When you get paid next week, we're gonna come back to see you and you're going to give us more of your tobacco.'

I felt the surge of anger creep over me. As he was talking, I slid the PP9 into my sock. Still smirking and stinking, he stepped back to leave. I should have run through the open door and shut them in. I should have rung the bell. Instead I tightened my fingers round the sock. In one movement I jumped off the bed, cracked him in the face with the PP9 and kicked the door shut. He fell to the floor and didn't get up again. Blood began to flow from above his eye. I turned to the other one, who started backing away. Only a lunatic would lock himself in a cell with two guys who were bigger than he was, but this was exactly the message I wanted to send.

I couldn't get out – but neither could they, so they knew I was going to fight. After rash-face had seen what I'd done to his mate, he started hitting the bell and kicking the door to get out. I punched him and kicked him over and over again. Even when I heard the screws running in, I didn't stop. They peeled me off him. I fought all the way to the punishment block, swearing, kicking, lashing out. They beat me and dumped me in the isolation cell. I heard the door clang shut and knew that I'd lost some remission. My knuckles were bleeding and my shoulder hurt, but I didn't care. I had sent my message loud and clear: don't mess with me. I heard later that I'd broken one guy's jaw and two of the other guy's ribs. They never bothered me again, and the rest of the inmates left me alone too.

It was the noise that nearly drove me over the edge – people shouting, screaming, doors banging. It was never quiet, and it fuelled my anger.

At night inmates would open their windows and shout at others in nearby cells.

'Oi you, number 42, come to the window now. If you don't come to the window now, in the morning I'll come in your cell, and you know what I'll do. Get to the window now!'

The reply would have an almost convincing lack of concern: 'Yeah, what do you want?'

'I done your mum before I came in here. I'm gonna do your girlfriend when I come out. I nicked her picture off your wall. I'm lookin' at her now: what you gonna do about it?'

And so it went on, day and night.

Isolation was my natural habitat. I'd been alone all my life – at school, at my parents' house, at Stamford House. I'd learned to deal with confinement in the isolation unit at Stamford House when I was ten. I'd had to. And so I chose the silence of the punishment block over the bedlam of the main wing. Here was one more way I could ensure the screws didn't win. I knew I could handle it. I started requesting to go. It drove the screws mad. When they refused to take me, I started fights – with them or another prisoner – and I got my stint in the punishment block. The longer they left me down there, the more I learned to endure it. Soon they didn't know whether they were punishing me or rewarding me. I was in control.

I started doing press-ups in isolation – the first day five, then ten, then fifteen. I'd do them until it hurt and then I'd do more, working through the pain. It was one more way of training myself to be immune, unbreakable. It was a physical battle but it was a mental one, too – preparing myself to shut off future pain, blocking out the past, disregarding the consequences.

I'd just come out again when Social Services sent me to a workingmen's hostel. There was a young black man working at reception. He was squinting at me.

'What you staring at?' I asked him.

'You don't remember me do you?'

'Nah, I don't.'

'I'm Mr Lewis.'

I shrugged.

'When I was training to be a social worker a few years ago, I had a placement in a secure unit. You were there. I remember because when you tried to burn the place down and we tried to restrain you, this is what you did.'

He turned his head. He only had half an ear.

'You bit it off,' he said.

I couldn't remember doing it. 'I don't know what you're talking about,' I mumbled and shuffled to my room.

Each time I was released, I had to replace the burgling tools that I'd disposed of or had confiscated at my arrest. It was a real inconvenience, and sometimes it was difficult to find just the right one. The knife I preferred for opening window catches was a flick-knife that enabled me to sheath the blade and carry it in my pocket. I smiled sometimes when I thought of my first kitchen knife.

One night when I was fifteen, fresh out of prison again, I sat behind a wall staking out a house. I'd had my eye on this house for a while. I never passed a house I didn't want to burgle, but this was going to be good. The guy was getting ready to go out, I could see him through the window. I was pretty sure he worked a night shift. I sat waiting, flicking my new knife in and out. It glinted in the moonlight. I pressed my thumb into its cold steel, wondering if I'd draw blood. The guy in the house turned out the light and I heard the door slam. I tensed. Then the light went on again. He'd forgotten something. I waited some more and I started thinking. What if he hadn't remembered whatever it was until he was halfway to work? What if he'd come back in the middle of my burglary? I stared down at the knife in my hand and I knew that if anyone got in my way, my knife would serve double duty as a weapon. I'd stab him.

That scared me.

In that moment I discovered a weak spot in all my training and discipline to feel nothing but anger. I was fifteen and I saw where my future lay. I stood up, shaking, and walked into the probation service.

'I can't stop what I'm doing,' I told the woman behind the counter. 'I need help.'

'What's your name?' she asked.

'Steve. Steve Cattell.'

'OK, Steve. What's the problem?'

'My whole life is going out, stealing and hurting people. Then I get locked up for it. As soon as I get out I start all over again. I hate it. I don't want to do it any more, but I don't know how to stop.'

'Steve,' she said to me, 'the only person who can make you stop is you.'

I walked out of there without hope. Three days later, I was back serving another sentence.

5

Sometimes I was on remand for months before my court date. There were other boys like me, constantly in and out of remand centres, and certain faces became as familiar as the bars on the windows and the back of the cell door. They weren't friends – we just did time together. We started to compete with each other – who could do the most time before actually being sentenced. Whoever went to court first had to give their fags to the rest of us, so when someone's court date came through, we could pretend to be pleased. We won, we had the cigarettes – so who really cared if we were stuck there indefinitely? Who cared if we faced any more time inside after finally being sentenced? I didn't.

Eight months was my longest time on remand. I always pleaded 'Not guilty.' I didn't have to do anything to try to avoid a custodial sentence – my social workers did it all for me. I just let them get on with it. When you're under sixteen, they do whatever they can on your behalf. They seemed so desperate for me to be released. I don't know why – maybe they believed prison wasn't the best place for me, maybe they were on commission – I didn't care why as long as I got out. I was desperate to be released, too – so I could continue burgling.

I'd served these eight months, and my court appearance was finally less than a week away, when my social worker came to see me. Anna-Marie was American and always wore bright pink lipstick – often on her teeth as well. It was nice to have a visit – whoever it was from. It felt good to be called by my first name – to the screws I was just another number. She stood with me outside my cell, holding her clipboard and watching people walk past. I looked at her security pass picture. She hadn't changed much since the picture was taken, still the same lipstick – maybe she looked older, more tired. When it was quiet she looked at me like she expected me to say something. I waited. My shoes were beginning to wear out – if I flexed my foot my big toe poked through the top of my left trainer.

'Look, Steve,' she sighed. 'I've read your file. I know how often you spend time in places like this. I believe . . . I believe you're incurable. You have an illness. You're incapable of changing. You're going to spend the rest of your life in prison.'

I didn't say anything. She had never spoken to me like this before. None of my social workers had spoken to me like this. She paused while some other prisoners walked past. I waited for her to continue.

'Steve, I've found a placement for you. It's with a guy called George. He's a professional thief. He's spent many years thieving. You don't like it here?'

I shook my head and stared at my trainers.

'OK, then you need to learn to be a better thief so you can stop getting caught. George can help you. At least then you can have some sort of life outside prison walls.'

I couldn't quite believe what I was hearing. I mumbled assent and wandered back into my cell.

George, it turned out, was about fifteen years older than me. He was a thief, but he was also a family man. He and his wife, Veronica, welcomed me into their three-bedroom flat. They had two young daughters, Charlotte and Elizabeth. We became very close. Both girls adopted me as their uncle. Sometimes Elizabeth refused to be read her bedtime story by her parents – she wanted Uncle Steve to do it. I wasn't great at reading, but her books were full of pictures and sometimes she'd want us to make up our own stories instead. There were twelve years between Charlotte and me, so although she called me her uncle I could have been her big brother. George had another daughter from an earlier marriage who we often saw as well. For the first time in my life, I felt that I was in a family and that I belonged.

George had grown up in the care system. He'd spent time in secure units and remand centres. He'd been through borstal. He understood me because he'd been exactly where I was. And Veronica had accepted George, knowing how he got his money, so there was a good chance she'd accept me. For the first time ever I could be honest about myself without risking a beating or a prison sentence. I didn't have to worry that they'd throw me out once they found out I liked to burgle houses – they already knew.

George was a controlled criminal. He planned and executed his crimes, while I just went out and did them. I didn't worry about what would happen if I got caught until I actually was. So I started to learn from him: how to use a crowbar properly, to wear gloves, what things to take from properties and where to sell them. George taught me that if you do a really tidy search, some people won't realise they've been burgled for days – sometimes weeks. Once he was satisfied I wouldn't drop him in it, he started taking me on jobs with him, mostly breaking into houses or warehouses.

We were never short of money. The flat we lived in was well furnished and Charlotte and Elizabeth had more toys and games than I'd had growing up. The rest of the money from the burglaries funded George and

Veronica's drug habit – they were both addicted to amphetamines and sulphate. It wasn't perfect. Sometimes they had violent fights. Sometimes I joined in. But I knew they'd be there for me. I don't know if they loved me, but they cared about me and that was enough. A family.

There was a house I often noticed on my way to the shops. It was a storey taller than the other houses on the street. It had a big wooden door with pillars on either side and loads of arched windows. I was sure it would be full of money and expensive jewellery. Every time I walked past it my fingers curled around the knife in my pocket. I often dreamed about popping open one of the windows and climbing through. I imagined that it looked like a palace inside. I showed the house to George. I thought we could do it together. I was sure we'd make loads.

George wasn't convinced. He pointed out the high railings and the big bolts on the door as well as the locked gate that made it difficult to get round the back. He demonstrated how anyone trying to break in would be seen from the road and from the windows of several of the other houses. He told me that it was too big a risk.

I tried to accept it. I tried to focus my mind on the job we were doing the next week on a warehouse on the other side of London instead. But every morning I woke up imagining the sound of the lock flicking back. Every night when I shut my eyes I could see it. I imagined getting in through the big wooden door, through the window, through a door at the back. I daydreamed about it. I fantasised about walking around inside that big fancy house being able to take anything I wanted. I imagined the sort of clocks and radios there would be, how I would find the jewellery box hidden at the back of a wardrobe – the feel of the cold expensive metal weighing my pockets down. If George wouldn't help me, I'd do it on my own.

I decided to do it the next day. I could barely hold in my excitement once I'd made the decision. I knew if I told George he'd try to stop me, so I kept quiet and tried to act normally. I packed a bag with my crowbar, torch and gloves and left it under my bed. I couldn't eat and I thought dinner would never be over. When it finally was, I grabbed my bag and told Veronica I was just nipping out and not to wait up. She was watching the end of a soap opera with Charlotte. She never asked me where I was going. I could hear my heart beating. I tried not to run as I headed for the house. There were no lights in the windows. I could almost smell the money.

Ten minutes later, I was handcuffed to a police officer. Twenty minutes later I was in the station, trying to explain the contents of my bag. Not only did I have a crowbar in it, but also a gold clock that had been on the mantelpiece in the big house.

After I answered 'No comment' to all of their questions, I got my borstal sentence (Young Offender's Institutes have now replaced borstals). I still had to march and call all the screws 'Sir,' but I was also supposed to learn a trade. I was given a job in the borstal greenhouse, growing tomatoes. The other inmate working in the greenhouse was called Kevin. He was there after burgling an electrical shop one night with some older lads. They'd made him get in first and pass them goods through the window. When the police came, they ran off, leaving Kevin still inside. He didn't even grass them up. I respected him for that.

The first week in borstal I fought almost continually. George had taught me how much easier life is if people are scared of you.

'If you want to make an impression,' he said, 'you need to do it immediately.'

So I did. I didn't care how much damage I did, as long as I won. I stopped fighting once people knew they couldn't take liberties with me and left me alone.

Working in the greenhouse was one of the better jobs. Cooped up in a cell, the closest I ever got to outside was staring through the bars on the window. I'd never had a visit in prison from anyone other than social workers, so it felt good when George and Veronica came to see me. They brought me a big bag of marijuana seeds as a present. I wasn't sure that they'd grow but, since I was working in the greenhouse, I decided to give it a try.

Kevin helped me plant the seeds in about thirty pots. It was a hot summer, so each day after watering them we took the pots round to the back of the greenhouse so that the natural sun could get to them. At night, before we had to go back to our wing, we put them back inside the greenhouse. We did this for about a week, but nothing seemed to be happening. We decided to keep trying for another couple of days and if they still weren't growing we'd chuck them away. That night I got into a fight with a guy in the snooker room and smashed the pool cue across his face, breaking his jaw. As usual I was sent to the punishment block. I was down there for two months of total silence. I wasn't allowed to talk to anyone, and a prison officer outside recorded everything. Although I'd learned to cope with isolation, it was harder during the summer, knowing I could have been working outside every day. It could have been any season in the block – any weather. Once again, my hatred for everyone and everything got me through. I forgot about everything else. When my two months were finally up, I'd been in my cell on the wing for less than half an hour when Kevin came tearing into my cell.

'Steve, they're all growing!'

'What?'

'The plants. They're growing!'

When I went out to the greenhouse the next day, I couldn't believe it. There were thirty shrubs about a foot high. What would George say? He'd done me a huge favour by bringing those seeds in. The most valuable currency in the borstal was tobacco. It paid for favours, bets, security – anything. The majority of the teenage inmates claimed to take drugs, although I doubted that was true. I looked at the marijuana plants. The leaves looked very similar to those on the tomato plants. If you didn't put them next to each other it would be difficult to tell the difference. Maybe no one else would know.

I picked all the leaves off the tomato plants and laid them on the hot pipes in the greenhouse. Once they were dry, I wrapped them up in half-ounce packets and sold them as marijuana. Lots of kids bought them. The next day, when we were unlocked, five boys came straight to my cell. I hadn't thought about what would happen when they found out what they'd bought wasn't marijuana, but it looked like I was about to. I clenched my fists and swung off my bunk. I didn't like my chances against five others, but I never back away from a fight.

'What do you want?' I demanded.

'More cannabis. We were off our faces last night.'

I waited to see if it was a joke. It wasn't. They'd come back to say what good stuff it was and how high they'd been and could they have some more. I couldn't believe it. I must have been the first person in the prison system to get half his borstal stoned on tomato leaves.

❖   ❖   ❖   ❖

I spent hours looking out of my cell window. I counted sixteen houses that I promised myself I'd burgle on my release. Planning future burglaries made the time pass more quickly. At night I allowed myself to imagine opening those locks, hearing the door close behind me. I felt the power of ownership over another property and everything in it. The anticipation was so real, it made me sweat. When my release date arrived, those houses were all I could think about. George picked me up from the prison.

'George, before we go back, I've seen some houses. I mean do we have time to . . .'

George smiled and reached into the back seat. He pulled out a bag containing gloves and my crowbar.

'No promises,' he said, 'but we'll have a look.'

One of them was set back from the road. The grass needed cutting and the letterbox was jammed with post. The lock broke easily.

'Hello!' I called out. 'Anyone here? You know your door's open.'

I relished the silence. It was so satisfying, even though I was disappointed by how little there was to take. I was finally doing what I'd been dreaming about for months. The most difficult part of being in prison, I realised, was being kept from doing the thing I loved more than anything else.

I stayed with George and Veronica for about a month. More and more I wanted to target bigger, more luxurious, houses, but George was not a risk taker. I began to resent his advice. After a big disagreement with George and Veronica, I left. I didn't have a fixed address. I didn't have many friends. Because I'd spent so much time in B & Bs and children's homes, drifting from place to place seemed normal. I kept in touch with George and Veronica, but I didn't go back to live with them. I was nearly seventeen –

I needed my independence. I ended up in a working-men's hostel.

The lonelier I felt, the more I isolated myself. Most of the people I met at the hostel were heavily into drugs. I started taking LSD, cannabis and amphetamines. They took my mind off things for a while but they were no sub-stitute for crime. Hate and violence and thieving were all I knew. They were my means of survival. Burgling didn't make me happy exactly, but it quenched my cravings for danger, excitement and adrenaline rushes, as well as money and power. So I continued to commit burglaries and found myself in and out of prison – mostly in, and rarely out for more than six weeks at a time.

6

It was my first night in Norwich Prison. I had just been sentenced to two months in custody for possession of stolen goods. The Young Offenders landing was full, so I was put downstairs in one of the hospital cells until a space became available for me. The cell, including the back of the door and the bed frame, was all pale green. Even the sheets matched. Most of the cells were unoccupied, so there weren't many screws around. It was almost as quiet as the punishment block. A smell of disinfectant lingered on everything – sometimes wafts of it came through the hatch on the door. All the cell doors on the hospital wing had a square hatch, about head-height, with bars across. Green bars. They'd been designed with flaps on the outside for the screws to pull up, but most of them were broken. So if the prisoner in the cell opposite looked through his hatch and I looked through mine we could see and talk to each other, even during lock down.

Nearby I heard a door crash shut, then footsteps fading away. The cell opposite me had been empty since I'd arrived that morning, but I looked through my hatch and thought I saw a movement.

'You all right mate?' I called out.

Nothing. I was sure I'd seen someone in there.

'Oi mate! You deaf or something?'

A face appeared at the opposite hatch – a big nose, black eyes, miserable. He looked about fifty, although it

was hard to tell through a little square in a door. I nodded at him.

'What's your name?' he asked in a quiet rasping
voice.

'Steve.'

'And how old are you Steve?'

'Seventeen.'

He stared at me. I wanted to look away but found I
couldn't. It was so quiet I could hear myself breathing.
He blinked.

'You know what, Steve? I'm forty-six tomorrow. I've
been in and out of prison all my life. It didn't bother me
especially. Probably like it doesn't bother you much at
the moment. Except last time I was out, I met this
woman. This wonderful woman. I fell for her. I couldn't
help it. I settled down and even got myself a job. I was
going straight. And it didn't matter that I didn't have
loads of money. I was happy. You listening, Steve?'

I nodded.

'Anyway, a robbery went off and the police fitted me
up. I never did it. I swear I never did it. But it didn't matter – I got done for it and now I've got seven years.
Seven years! I was going straight. I'm telling you now,
Steve – this is it. I've had enough of all of it. I'm not
going to do this any more.'

I didn't know what to say to him. I wasn't expecting
him to pour his heart out. I didn't even know his name.

'Cheer up mate, it's your birthday tomorrow,' I said.
And I went to bed.

The alarms woke me. For a moment I forgot where I
was. My back ached from lying on a thin mattress. My
eyes rested on the sink and toilet nailed to the floor. I
was back inside again. And that smell – disinfectant –
Norwich hospital wing. The alarms went on and on.
Something must have happened because it was before

six a.m. – the usual wake-up call. I threw back my sheet and went to the hatch. Through the square I watched as prison officers opened the door opposite mine. I could see straight in to the cell.

He was lying on the bed with the blanket over him. The floor was flooded red. I never knew the human body could produce so much blood. The yellow foam mattress was stained black-red. Soon, blood-footprints covered the landing as prison officers rushed in and out of his cell. They wheeled him out on a trolley, zipped up in a black body bag. After he'd finished talking to me, he'd cut his wrists, laid under his blanket and quietly bled to death. I could smell the blood.

One of the screws saw me watching through my hatch. If it hadn't been broken the screws would have shut it so I couldn't see what was happening. Instead, he asked me to go in there to mop the cell. I told him what he could do with his mop. I watched them clean up the cell and replace the mattress and the bedding. By lunchtime there were no traces of the man I'd spoken to. A few hours later they put someone else in the cell.

Some of the older prisoners organised a whip-round to buy the dead man a wreath. We could sign how much of our wages we wanted to contribute and it would be deducted. The man who came to collect from me had tattoos all the way up his arm and a massive gut.

'How much are you going to give?'

'I dunno. What are you getting him a wreath for? It's not like he's the first guy to die in this place.'

'Because he had courage. He decided what he wanted to do and saw it through. An awful lot of people cut their wrists in prison, but they can't go through with it and they ring the bell. They're too scared or they just want attention. He wanted to end his life so he cut his wrists and died with dignity.'

'Fair enough. I'll sign out a quid.'

It seemed right. He was well known there – Norwich was his local prison and he'd been in and out of it all his life. I heard later that someone else was arrested for the robbery he'd been charged with. He would have been acquitted.

When I finished that sentence, George and Veronica put me up at their flat until I got arrested again and was sent to a borstal in Kent for twenty-two months. I was prepared to spend the first week or so fighting, to establish my reputation in the new place. On the third day, a fight got out of control and I was sent to the punishment block. After three days of fighting, it was good to have a break on my own.

The screw opened the door after two weeks.

'Hey, thanks,' I told him. 'I enjoyed my little holiday from the wing. Mind if I stay a bit longer?'

He kicked the door shut.

If we leave him down there long enough we'll break him, they must have decided. That'll show him to stop asking to be sent there. I thought they might leave me down for a month.

Twelve weeks later I was still there. Twelve weeks not being allowed to talk; twelve weeks sitting on a three-legged stool made from cardboard so I couldn't do any damage with it; twelve weeks with one book.

Veronica's sister, Sue, sent me a letter. I didn't know her that well, but she used to visit the flat sometimes and she was a nice-looking girl. Her letter said she was sorry I was in prison and she was looking forward to me coming out. It felt good getting a letter like that – even though the screws took it off me once I'd read it. We weren't allowed to keep letters in isolation.

I could deal with all of that, though. I'd trained myself well. But it was torture not having any idea how long.

When would my time be up? Every morning at ten, I stood at the door as the governor walked by.

'Good morning.'

The governor looked at me and asked the screw, 'Yes, and how's Cattell been behaving?'

'Well Guv'nor, he was talking last night.'

And the door shut and I knew it would be at least another twenty-four hours before I might be able to go back to the wing. Twelve weeks in isolation, not knowing when it was going to end, was beginning to wear me down. I was bored and it was my eighteenth birthday. I decided to try a little bit of psychology. I had a few cards that had been sent in to me, including one from Sue, and I had been allowed to keep them for the day. I put them up where I knew the governor would see them as soon as the door opened. At ten I was ready at the door.

'Good morning, Guv'nor.'

'Name and number?'

'Cattell, B27744.'

'Yes and how's Cattell's behaviour?'

'Listen Guv'nor, it's my birthday today. I've been here three months now and I feel that I'm ready to go back to the wing. I'd like the chance to earn back some of the remission that I've lost. I've definitely learned my lesson.'

He looked at me for a few seconds. Then he smiled. 'Well, I don't think you've been down here long enough.'

As he turned to go, I picked up the three-legged stool and smashed him across the back of the head with it. The door swung shut. I heard the heavy lock being turned. About four hours later several officers steamed in and gave me the beating I'd been waiting for.

It was another six months before I was finally allowed back onto the wing. As I was being led up, someone shouted over the railings to me:

'Alright Steve? Glad to have you back. D'you wanna fag?'

I opened my mouth, but the only thing that came out was a faint noise from the back of my throat. After nine months of silent isolation, it was a couple of weeks before I could speak normally again.

I was given a trustee's job and placed on report for about six months. I'd quite enjoyed my short stretches in isolation until that long one. I knew another nine months down there would kill me, so I kept my head down and got on with the job – I even started to enjoy the responsibility. I managed a couple of months without any trouble so I went to the Governor to ask if I could get back some of the remission I'd lost. He looked at me for a while, like he had when he'd visited me in isolation. When he spoke, his voice was quiet.

'You aren't getting anything back. The reason I gave you a trustee's job was I figured it might keep you out of trouble. I don't want you here – I thought if we just left you alone that perhaps you'd hurry up and get out of this establishment. But that's it. You are not about to get any privileges.'

When I did finally get out of his establishment, George was at the gate to pick me up. Initially I went back to the workingmen's hostel but was soon back living with George and Veronica. A few days after my release, George and I drove by a factory with some cardboard boxes outside. Neither of us knew what the place was so we stopped to have a look. We discovered that the factory made LPs and the boxes outside were seconds to be sent back for melting. George and I decided to take them and sell them on – maybe open a record shop.

Every day we went to the factory and stole five boxes, each containing a hundred records. We sold them for half the retail price. We opened two stalls in Portobello Road and two in Petticoat Lane. We were in business for about a year and the money was unbelievable. The average wage at the time was about fifteen pounds per week, but I was earning up to eight hundred pounds a week from the records alone – money from any burglaries I did was extra. George had taught me how to tell if a mortice lock was on or off by looking at it. I became so good at it I could drive by a house with a mortice lock and have a good idea whether it was on or not. If it looked off, I'd pick out a landmark nearby so I could return the next day with my crowbar and a bag to fill. Between the record business and burglaries, I had more money than I could spend.

I was driving a Lotus sports car, flashing my money and enjoying the buzz. The police were taking notice of my prosperity, but I paid off bent policemen who arrested me so I'd get bail. The best thing money bought me was power. I stayed out of prison for almost a year and I was gaining respect within the criminal world. I started seeing Veronica's sister, Sue. She knew I was a criminal, but I think she thought she could change me. At eighteen I had my own place, a fast car, and a good-looking girl on my arm. I should have been happy. Eventually, I had another disagreement with George and our working relationship dissolved.

The first time I met Stan was in his local, a pub opposite his flat. A mutual acquaintance introduced us, so I was fairly certain he was a criminal. We got talking and he told me he'd lost all his money in a betting shop that day. I'd had a good day and had a few grand. Stan seemed like a good bloke so I gave him a couple of hundred quid. When I went into the toilet I caught him stuffing the money into his sock. It was already bulging with notes. He wasn't skint; he just found another person to con. I was mad he had conned me – but we were both thieves. We had that in common. Stan would con anyone. He'd love you but he'd also rob you.

I had spent long enough in the criminal world to know that crooks don't have friends – they have mates; acquaintances they do jobs with. But if one of my mates knew that I had twenty grand in a drawer in my house, he wouldn't think twice about coming round and nicking it. Just like I wouldn't think twice about nicking it from him. It's survival of the fittest. I knew I had to be sharper than the bloke I was working with. When I did a burglary with someone else, I had to keep my eyes open, because if he found a jewellery box, half of it would go down his trousers and he'd only declare the other half. I've heard the saying 'There's honour among thieves,' but I've never found it to be true.

So, mad as I was at Stan for conning me, I hung around and got to know him. We often went for a few drinks at his local after a hard day of burgling. Stan made his living as a tout up the West End. He'd take people into doorways and offer them a good time with a girl upstairs. If they were interested, he'd take their money – anything from twenty to a hundred quid – and he'd disappear around the corner. Of course there wasn't anyone upstairs; he was just a con merchant. He'd return to the doorway a couple of hours later and wait for another punter. It was a good scam as his disappointed customers were hardly going to report it to anybody.

Since splitting with George I worked mostly on my own, but Stan and I did occasional jobs together and while I was on the run from the police Stan put me up on and off for several months. Whatever I'd done, he never turned me away. He was one of the only people who was always there for me. He was a good thief, and he was also a compulsive drinker and gambler.

I liked the occasional bet, but I'd never been into it in a big way – until I met Stan. He introduced me to the illegal card shops in the West End, casinos and betting shops. Many of the gamblers were drug dealers, armed robbers and shoplifters. These people accepted me. Gambling, especially when the stakes were high, gave me a fantastic buzz – similar to the buzz of breaking into a house – and I became addicted. There's only so much you can spend on clothes, women, holidays and cars, so gambling gave me something else to burgle for. Before I met Stan, I went to nightclubs and spent a few hundred on drinks and girls. But I could put a grand on a horse and it would be gone in seconds. The bigger the bet, the better the buzz.

The bigger the bets, the more money I needed to fund my lifestyle. I began to do jobs with people I met in the gambling dens. I picked more expensive, riskier premises for burgling. It wasn't long before I found myself in prison again.

7

Despite our arguments, George and Veronica were the best family I'd known. I didn't know much, but I knew that I wanted whatever it was they had together for myself. I'd also learned ·from talking to other criminals that having a wife meant more lenient sentences. I'd been seeing Sue for about a year when I proposed and she accepted. I was on bail at the time for conspiracy to rob. I decided to get a job for her sake – working increased my chances of getting off without being taken into custody.

I found a job in a textile warehouse and kept out of prison. At the end of the year there was almost a million pounds worth of stock missing. My pay was forty pounds a week and I was stealing four hundred pounds worth of material per day and selling it on. Sue and I enjoyed the lifestyle this income provided, and some of the money went towards our wedding. As the textile company continued to lose money, however, they had to let some workers go. I was one of them.

Being married and even employed didn't mean that I no longer needed to be unbreakable. I never let up on the personal training regime I began in Ashford Remand Centre – smashing my hands into walls and burning myself in cups of tea. Every day I had Sue strike my chest and stomach with an iron bar and I forced myself to endure it without crying out. My goal was to be totally immune to pain.

Once I lost my job at the textile factory, I brainstormed other ways to make money. I thought back to my days in care when I stayed in the B & Bs at Finsbury Park. My next-door neighbours were prostitutes, alcoholics or unmarried mothers in temporary accommodation. I remembered noticing that a lot of giros would come through every Thursday. I'd never stolen giros before and I was used to being out of prison, so I knew I had to be careful, like George, if I wanted to stay out.

I booked into four B & Bs in the Finsbury Park area and got the outdoor keys cut. I returned the originals and booked out. The following Thursday morning, about half past seven, I sat on the wall of the first one and watched until I could see the postman coming. I let myself in with my new key and waited behind the door.

As the mail came through, I shoved it down my trousers then went round the corner, pulled all the giros out and put the rest of the post back. People might then think they would come in the second post rather than assume they were missing. It seemed to work, so I did the same at the other three B & Bs. That first Thursday, I made just short of three thousand pounds, and every week after that for about a year, until the system changed to over-the-counter payments and giros were no longer sent out. It was easy to cash the giros. All I had to do was get rent books from WH Smith's and fill them out in the name of the person on the giro in case they asked for identification. There were no codes, so I could cash them at any post office.

Then, one day, as I was driving home after a hard day's work in a stolen car with my giros, I glanced in the wing mirror and saw a policeman on a motorcycle riding up behind me. Fast. And all of a sudden I was seeing double. There was another one on my other side, trying to pull me over. I swerved and watched the carnage in the rear-view mirror. I'd knocked one of them off his bike. This was exhilarating! I spun round the corner, tyres screeching.

I looked up and saw them but I didn't ask myself, 'Steve, should you stop for this roadblock?' I wasn't about to stop. I mounted the pavement, smashed through two police cars and crashed into a wall. I swung out, unhurt and ready to run.

They had me cuffed and back in prison faster than I could cash a giro.

The exhilaration of the police chase awoke my need for danger, and I couldn't wait to get out so I could go back to committing riskier crimes. So when I was arrested again, it was for burglary and I got three years – my longest sentence so far – in Wormwood Scrubs. Three years was a life-sentence for burglary. It was a deterrent sentence.

I was sitting on my bunk bed in Wormwood one day while my cellmate did press-ups. He was a big strong guy and he exercised all day, every day. I just wanted to sit quietly, read a book and do my time. I tried to shut out the grunts and the smell of sweat so I could concentrate on what I was reading. I couldn't.

'Listen, mate. You have to stop that because the cell is starting to smell. We've got nothing here for you to have a bath in or anything and it's disgusting.'

'Shut up,' he snarled.

I watched him for a moment; he was massive. I was tall, but I was skinny – I couldn't fight him and win. There was a modelling knife on the table that he'd made from two razor blades set into a toothbrush. I got off the bed, picked up the knife and slashed his throat. Simple. It bloodied the ceiling and the walls. I felt calm. I watched him sway and gag. I reached onto my bunk, picked up a towel and chucked it at him.

'If you're gonna die, then go over and die in the corner. Just don't die over me.'

He managed to hit the bell, and the screws came and dragged him to the hospital. They saved his life and took me to the punishment block. While he was in the hospital wing he made a statement against me. Initially I was to be charged with attempted murder, but it got dropped to GBH. I had four mates in the prison, all doing time for armed robbery. They got hold of him in the exercise yard while I was in the punishment block. They threatened that if he didn't shut his mouth and retract his statement they would finish the job I'd started.

He did what he was told and the charges were dropped.

Because of what I'd done, they transferred me from the Scrubs to Camp Hill Prison on the Isle of Wight. I spent seven days on the induction wing while the prison went through my files and observed me so they could allocate me a wing. That first night, they opened up all the cells for showers but left me locked. Then they opened up all the cells for an hour of TV but left me locked. I hadn't done anything; I'd just arrived. I kicked the door until the screw finally came.

'Why haven't you opened me for a shower?' I demanded. 'You've opened everyone else.'

'You'll have to wait 'til next week then, won't you.'

'Why couldn't I watch TV?'

'I must have forgot to open you.'

The next day, standing in front of the governor, I understood. The governor of Camp Hill was the same man who had been the governor of my borstal in Kent – the one whose head I'd smashed with a stool. I knew there was no point kicking up a fuss. As time went on, things got worse. Within three months I'd lost eleven months of remission. The screws kept leaving me locked up and were constantly getting at me.

'Cattell. You haven't had a shave this morning.'

'No. I've got a shaving rash and I can't shave.'

'OK, so the doctor has said that you can't then?'

'Well if you look at my face you will see that I'm covered in a shaving rash and I can't shave because it'll make it worse.'

'OK, you're on report.'

That cost me seven days remission and a stint down the block. I came back, saw the same officer, and refused to shave again. I lost another seven days remission with three days in solitary. I came back again, still refused, and lost another seven days remission with another three days in solitary confinement with no furniture and no fags. When I returned, the same officer was waiting and smiling.

'So Cattell, are you going to make it fourth time lucky?'

There was a tea urn next to me. It was full with steam coming out of the top. I grabbed it, flung its contents into his face and went for him. Within seconds all the other screws arrived. They kicked me and beat me and threw me back in the punishment block in a straight jacket. It didn't bother me – I found it funny, which just made them madder.

'I ain't been found guilty yet, have I? I can't be done for anything until the guv'nor sees me tomorrow, so you just keep kicking the shit out of me but I want my fags!'

I went back to the wing only once more after that, and while I was there I went for a screw with a razor blade. After that incident they sent a psychiatrist from Parkhurst to have a look at me. I was, he declared, 'a danger to prison officers and unfit to go back into mainstream prison.' That meant isolation for the rest of my sentence. Eighteen months.

It was a very lonely year and a half. I marked off one day on my calendar and the next thing I knew it was seven days – nothing had changed, nothing had happened, every day exactly like the next and the one before it. The prison officers tormented me by knocking on doors as they went past. A previous inmate had drawn a topless woman on the wall in biro. There was nothing else to look at in that cell and I can remember every line, every curve of that drawing in detail, as well as all the filthy messages that other prisoners had scrawled round it. On the opposite wall brown mould bubbles pushed through the paintwork like some kind of evil.

The punishment block's principal officer spent the entire eighteen months trying to break me. My furniture was cardboard . . . cardboard table, cardboard chair. I had to put the bed outside during the day, but I used to turn the table over on its side and sit or lie behind it, so anyone looking through the Judas flap in the door couldn't see me. When the officer checked my cell I'd stick my hand up from behind the table and give a little wave, 'Still here!' Man, they hated that and it made me laugh. I spent every day behind that table.

They'd open the door and say, 'Exercise, Cattell.'

'No thank you,' I'd wave. 'Goodbye.'

'Put up your table,' they'd order me.

'No. Why should I? What are you going to do? Take my table? If you take my table I'll just sit over there behind the door so when you look through your little flap you won't even be able to see my hand. You won't even know if I'm alive or dead.'

I got a letter from Sue while I was down there. She'd met someone else. I didn't love her, but it really upset me. I was twenty-two, I looked at the same four walls twenty-four hours a day, and I felt disrespected – knowing that some other man was in my home having sex with my wife.

The nights were the hardest. I knew I was breakable when I was totally alone in the dark. I fell to the floor on my knees and screamed and prayed for the devil. I knew the devil was anger, hate and evil – and I was all three. I needed him, his hate and anger, to get me to the next day. The god manipulating and controlling evil is Satan, and I lived in his world of evil and he was my god.

Anger and hatred strengthened me inside. The only thing that got me through that sentence was the hate and the anger I felt towards the human race. I couldn't wait to get out and attack society, to inflict as much pain as possible.

On New Year's Eve, about midnight, I heard bells ringing and inmates shouting out the windows. I laid in my cell thinking about how next New Year's Eve I wouldn't be lying on this bed. I would be out. I fantasised about flicking back a mortice lock with my crowbar and entering an empty house. The owners would be out celebrating while I helped myself to their stuff.

Dead on twelve o'clock there was a rustling at the door. I got out of bed. A piece of paper had been shoved under the door. I took it to the window where the light of a street lamp was just about bright enough to read it.

YOU HAVE BEEN REFUSED YOUR PAROLE.

The principal officer must have held that note for a couple of days so he could give it to me as a New Year greeting.

Seven days of home leave before release was a statutory right for prisoners doing three years or more. After Sue left me for someone else, I decided the leave was probably to go home to beat the crap out of the bloke who's taken your wife. I applied for leave over and over again but never got it. I used to advise people to take home leave as close to the end of their sentence as possible – there's nothing worse than having a week at home and then having to go back to prison for another six months. Prisoners with three weeks or less of their sentences left are allowed to apply for short-term home leave, which is a weekend. I never bothered applying for that, so I didn't believe it when a screw offered it to me.

'Cattell. Do you want to go home for the weekend?'

'Is this a wind up?'

'No. Your application for home leave was refused because you're into the last three weeks of your sentence, but you've been granted a weekend's statutory home leave.'

'I'll take it.'

Although Sue had left and was living with her new bloke, she was good to me even while I was still inside. She kept our flat and paid the rent and the other bills so I'd have a place to come home to. One of the conditions of my home leave was that I stayed in Stevenage, Hertfordshire with my sister-in-law, Veronica. As soon as I got out, however, I went straight to London, breaking my licence. Sue met me to hand over the keys for the flat. The first thing I did was ring Camp Hill Prison.

'Camp Hill Prison, can I help you?'

'Could I speak to the governor please?'

'Who's speaking?'

'Steven Cattell.'

The governor came on the line, 'Ah, Mr Cattell, you've only been out five hours, what seems to be the problem?'

'You're the problem. I thought I'd let you know I'm sitting in my flat in Islington drinking a cup of tea, and I ain't comin' back to you or your prison ever again.'

'You're where?'

'You heard me.'

'You get yourself back here now. If you're in London you've broken the terms of your licence.'

'Come back? You must be having a laugh. I ain't going back there. Ever. You beat me, kept me in the block for eighteen months, you victimised me. You can forget it. You ain't never gonna see me again.'

I put the phone down and sat there looking at the receiver for a while. Then I got up and made myself another cup of tea. I plunged my hand into it and it felt great – no pain. I stayed in the flat a couple of weeks until the police came and arrested me. I knew they'd take me to a local London prison to finish the remainder of my sentence – I didn't have long left to serve. I figured I'd lose some remission for failing to return, but it wouldn't be anything like Camp Hill. After four days in the new prison, I was taken to stand in front of the governor. He told me I'd lost three days remission and a week's wages and he sent me back to the wing. Ever since I'd seen the psychiatrist at Camp Hill, I'd been given cells on my own. That suited me just fine.

Soon I had only eight days left.

'Pack up your kit, Cattell,' a screw ordered as he opened the cell door.

'Why?'

'You're going down to the punishment block.'

'What for? I haven't done anything.'

'I don't know. You'll have to find out when you're down there.'

The punishment block screw assigned me a cell. 'I just don't get it,' he muttered, shaking his head.

'What?'

'I've been down this block over twenty years and I've never seen what's happened this morning.'

I yawned. 'What's that then?'

'Your old governor has been on the phone all morning to our governor. He wants you back on the next bus to Camp Hill. Our governor is asking what the point is of sending you back for seven days. But their governor wants you back. Our governor is refusing to send you back, so they've reached a mutual agreement that you get re-punished. Three days in the punishment block. Twenty years,' he shook his head again, 'I've never known a prisoner to be punished twice for the same offence.'

He looked at me then and handed me my radio, my bed, my cigarettes and my books.

'I'm not going to be a party to punishing somebody twice for the same crime. It's not right.'

So I spent my most luxurious three days ever in the punishment block. And I smiled every time I thought of how Camp Hill's governor would fume if he could see me.

8

Although we bumped into each other now and again, I hadn't heard from Stan for a while. I knew he'd still put me up if I needed it, but we rarely worked together. He was almost always drunk and we'd started to mix in different circles. So I was surprised when he rang me up one night.

'Here Steve. You'll never believe this. I'm going on the QE II next week.'

'You're what?'

'I'm serious! There's this guy, who was a close friend of my mum's before she died. He's come into an inheritance. And he's only gone and booked me a passage for a round the world trip with him.'

'The real QE II?'

'It'd better be. He paid eight grand for it.'

My mind was racing. This opportunity was too good to miss.

'Listen Stan, those cruise ships are packed with rich old ladies. See if you can find one with loads of jewellery we can sell and I'll get you off that boat at the next port and we'll split it, yeah?'

'OK, Steve. Steve?'

'Yeah?'

'I've saved up two thousand, seven hundred quid for this trip – from shoplifting. It's taken me five weeks. I've put it in the building society and everything.'

'Whatever, Stan.'

Stan had been away for three days when I received an urgent message to phone him on the QE II. When I finally got through, he sounded anxious.

'I can't talk now, but you've got to get me off this boat. We're docked in New York so sort me out a flight from there.'

I wondered how much he'd managed to steal. I booked a flight leaving New York the next day and arriving in London the day after. When I called to give him the flight information, he still refused to talk. He thanked me and hung up. I assumed someone was on to him, so I waited a couple of days for a phone call once he was back in England. When I didn't hear anything I called round his flat. He was swaying and reeking of whisky as he opened the door.

It turned out he'd spent all the money he'd saved in the boat's onboard casino. He'd blown nearly three grand in two days and had nothing left for the rest of the trip. The man who'd bought Stan's ticket continued on the cruise alone.

I didn't see him for a while after that. I was angry that he'd blown the chance to make some serious money, and the police caught up with me for some burglaries and I ended up back in custody.

During my next short stretch of freedom, I met Roz. She had three children from a previous marriage, and one of the things that attracted me about Roz was that I figured no one would want her and the kids while I was inside – unlike Sue. With Roz I'd be sure to have someone to come home to when I was released. I never bothered to hide my criminal lifestyle from her, and within months we were married.

I'd promised her a holiday to Gran Canaria, and the day before we left I sauntered into the bedroom to watch her pack. The case was open on the bed and summer clothes were laid out all over the room.

I flicked through the contents of the case. 'Oi, Roz,' I said. 'You've forgotten to pack something.'

'What's that?'

'The crowbar.'

'On holiday?'

'Of course on holiday,' I said. I showed her my pride and joy – a specially made crowbar that could open most locks with very little leverage.

She wasn't impressed that I insisted on packing a crowbar under the swimwear and suntan lotion. While Roz lay in the sun drinking sangria and getting sunburn, I levered open apartment after apartment. I had enough money for the holiday before we left. I had enough money for when I came home. Most people go on holiday to get away from work, but most people don't love their job like I loved mine. Just like I couldn't go away without my cigarettes, there was no way I could go on holiday without my fix of criminal activity. It was part of my life – eat, drink, sleep, steal – at home or abroad.

One weekend after we got back Roz and I went to Argos in Stoke Newington. Opposite the Argos was a place called The Front Line, a café swarming with Jamaicans doing drugs and gambling. White people wouldn't go in because they wouldn't come out alive. As I started pulling out in my car, a black guy drove up in his and blocked me. He was talking to a crowd of about ten Jamaicans on the street outside the café – he hadn't noticed I was there. I sounded my horn and gestured for him to move. He turned and started yelling abuse at me. I felt my hands tighten round the steering wheel. He carried on shouting and threatening. I threw open the car door and jumped out. In the boot of my car was a bag of tools. I pulled out my chisel, marched over to his car and sliced his ear off. It was a mess. Blood everywhere and all over the interior of his fancy car. There was a second of silence. No one moved. Then the Jamaicans on the pavement all started throwing bottles at me and my car.

'I have a lady in there,' I yelled. 'She's not involved in this fight. I am. I'm going to take her home and I'll be back.'

The whole journey home, Roz begged me not to go back. I walked her into the house, picked up my machete and got back in the car. I don't know if she tried to follow me: I didn't look in the wing mirror. I drove straight back to Stoke Newington, kicked open the door of the café and raised the machete above my head.

'Right, which of you wants to lose their head? Which one of you threw the bottle at the car? If you all want to come at me, come at me. I want to die. And if I'm going to die, I'm going to bring you all with me.'

The only sound was a fan whirring in the corner. They knew only a lunatic who was going to do exactly what he said he was going to do would come into a place with a hundred Jamaicans all armed with guns and knives. I returned home unscathed.

It was around this time that I started doing jobs with drug addicts. I stole bank details from houses and sent a female addict into the bank with the information to withdraw cash. Often the addicts checked how much was there first. They worked for me because they needed money to buy the drugs they needed. I became a master at manipulating addicts, mixing kindness and threats.

One woman I was working with went in to the bank with some stolen account details to check the balance.

'Steve,' she said when she came back to my car, 'there's twenty grand in the account. How much should I take?'

'Take ten grand.'

'I can't. That'll be too suspicious.'

'Shut your mouth and take it. Just get in there and take ten grand. You do what you're told. I supply the bankbooks – you go in there and do your job. This is what I pay you for. Now get in there.'

Drug addicts generally only wanted to withdraw five or six hundred, enough money for their drugs. I wanted the money to finance my lifestyle. I made sure they took out what I told them to take out. If they came out with ten grand and said, 'That was so sweet. They just paid me out,' I'd say, 'Right, at one o'clock when that counter lady goes to lunch you go back in there and get the other ten.'

That's how I worked. I controlled them by controlling the money for the drugs that controlled them. That's power – a power of control no different from a pimp controlling his girls on the street. I could take what I wanted. I could do what I wanted.

Roz and I lasted about three years and had a kid together, Shane. But we broke up while I was serving yet another custodial sentence. The prison system at the time was closing its gates for industrial action and Pentonville was the only one in London that was accepting prisoners. Pentonville usually took prisoners serving twelve-month sentences or less but, due to the situation, I was admitted for a four-year stretch. Prison was what I did between burglaries. The more time I spent in prison the less effect it had on me. Sometimes, when I'd had enough of my cellmate or I wanted to wind up the screws, I packed my kit and waited for the screw to come and open the door.

'What are you doing, Cattell?'

'I've had enough of this. I'm going down the block for a few weeks.'

They hated that I chose to be there, because when they wanted to send me there as a punishment they knew it would have no effect. They always refused to take me to the punishment block for doing nothing wrong.

'Look,' I'd say to the screw. 'You can take me down there for no reason, or I'll give you a reason.'

That was usually enough to guarantee me a stay of a couple of weeks. Every day, every hour in isolation made me stronger. After eighteen months in isolation, I could take anything. No one and nothing could touch me.

I never tried to make friends, but during this stretch I got to know another prisoner called Paul. He was serving twenty-one months for offences related to obtaining heroin. He was in his early twenties but he looked older. I could see the early signs of a drug addict in his face. He could hold his own in a fight though, and most people didn't want to mess with the skinhead with the pale blue eyes and the gold tooth. Paul and I had things in common. He had never known his father and was brought up in children's homes until he was eighteen. We both kept to ourselves inside, but we both had violent tempers. I backed Paul up in the few fights he got into, and he did the same for me. We did enough damage to ensure a reputation amongst the other inmates so we'd be left alone. We both had our controlling obsessions, too: Paul's was heroin; mine was crime.

After I'd been at Pentonville about six months the other prisons started admitting again. Paul left, along with all the other inmates serving more than a year. I'd just gone up for my first parole paper and I had the option to stay there until my parole was reviewed. Once my parole had started, I was the only prisoner there serving more than twelve months. As a result I had a single cell, the only one on the wing.

After Paul left, I didn't get to know anyone else. Most of the other inmates were small-time criminals and I think I intimidated them. One afternoon we were unlocked and a new prisoner, a big man, came to my door. I'd seen him pushing his weight around.

'Oi Cattell. I've heard you've had a visit. You've got some drugs in, yeah? Any chance of giving us some for tonight?'

'No.'

'What?'

'No. None at all. I don't like you. You slapped a geezer yesterday who couldn't fight back. You're a bully. Why don't you come into my cell and try and slap me? Because I hit back, mate.'

He looked me up and down, turned, and swaggered back to his cell. I found out his name was Clive, and a week later he was back, standing in my doorway.

'I've been asking around and you know what? I'd never fight you, Cattell – ever.'

'Why's that?' I asked.

'Because I'd be frightened to turn my back,' Clive snarled.

'Yeah, you'd be right too.' I leaned towards him. 'You know exactly what you'd get.'

I didn't have to spell it out. He knew I could put him in a wheelchair. More importantly, he knew I would. My philosophy was this: when I stood up to people who tried to intimidate me, we ended up with a mutual respect. Clive knew that if he started on me I'd have stabbed him before his back was turned, and I'd go for the spinal cord.

I wasn't about to walk the streets watching my back, knowing that someone who wouldn't think twice about killing me was walking free. The simple logic is, put him in a wheelchair so he's not capable of doing it. Clive and I got on all right after that – once we understood each other. Or, I should say, once he understood me.

Anger controlled and propelled my every action. I didn't care if I died. I did whatever I had to do. I became immune to prison.

After almost four years in Pentonville I came out with nothing: no money, no house, no relationship. I went into that sentence a burglar, but I came out a very dangerous man. I wanted the expensive lifestyle I'd had before I was arrested, and I wanted it immediately. I knew one or two burglaries wouldn't be enough. I needed more. So, the next time I went out, I got a gun.

I had information about some wealthy people who were holding vast amounts of money at their house. I went to the address and rang the bell. As the door began to open I muscled in, grabbed the man and shoved my gun down the back of his throat.

'Who is it darling?'

A woman appeared at the top of the upstairs. When she saw me she started to scream.

'Shut up right now or I'll shoot him,' I shouted.

She stopped.

'Where's the money?'

I hit the guy in the face with the gun until he was bleeding and almost fainting. He gestured with his eyes upstairs. I made the woman go first and followed behind, pulling the man by his hair. She led me to a room that was being used like a storeroom. Against the wall was a large safe with a number code. The couple whimpered as I tied them up.

'What's the number? Tell me or I'll shoot!' I waved the gun at the man's head.

'Please, my husband's got a heart condition.'

'I don't care if he's got a heart condition. I don't care if you both die, but you do it after you tell me the number to the safe.'

I really didn't care, and I was prepared to pull the trigger if I had to. All I cared about was leaving the house with what I came for – the money. Having a gun in my hand just made it easier. The whole thing took about ten minutes. I went back to the B&B where I was staying with just under a hundred thousand pounds – enough for a sports car, a wardrobe full of clothes and a return to the lifestyle to which I had become accustomed.

I was progressing up the ladder of the criminal world, committing crimes with people older than myself. After the armed robbery, I received lots of offers for that type of work – bank robberies and other higher-grade crimes – most of which I declined. Armed robbers tend to go out once a month and live off the proceeds; I wanted to commit crimes every single day. Gun crime didn't give me the same buzz. It was over too fast. I preferred burglaries because they gave me the adrenaline rush. But with that armed robbery I broke through a barrier of fear. I no longer feared anything or anyone. I didn't need anyone. I had my anger and my hate and my obsession. I wasn't interested in a relationship after two failed marriages. One-night stands were enough for me.

Although I'd all but lost contact with George, I still thought about him sometimes. He'd been the closest thing I'd had to a father. I hadn't seen the family for a few months when Veronica rang to tell me that George had died. I was gutted. Apparently he'd had a heart attack from the sustained use of amphetamines. I couldn't imagine how Veronica would cope without him. Breaking up with Sue hadn't affected my relationship with my sister-in-law. After George died, I started popping in to see Veronica and the girls almost every week. Just to make sure they were all right. Elizabeth, their youngest daughter, still called me Uncle Steve.

The Christmas Eve after George died, Veronica phoned me.

'Steve, Charlotte's in hospital,' she sobbed.

'What? What's happened? Veronica?'

'Please, Steve, please.' I could barely make out what she was saying.

'OK, Veronica, it'll be OK. I'll be there as soon as I can.'

When I arrived at the hospital, I learned that Charlotte had taken an ecstasy tablet that had sent her into a coma. I sat by her bedside all night long, holding her hand and telling her everything would be all right. It was difficult to believe that this girl wired up to all those machines was the same little girl I'd grown up with.

On Christmas morning the hospital pronounced her dead. Veronica refused to accept it and made them keep her alive for another three months before the machines were finally switched off.

No one I knew in the criminal world ever died of old age. It was always drugs, suicide or murder. Charlotte was fifteen.

9

It was a Thursday night. I was driving home in the pouring rain with a boot full of stolen gear. One of my windscreen wipers broke, and when I pulled over I realised I was just a hundred metres from a pub I recognised – Stan's local. I hadn't seen him for a few years but I decided to go in for a drink until the rain let up.

Stan was there, slumped at the bar and staring at nothing, his fingers clutching at the bar towel. He was a mess. His skin was yellow and, when I called his name, he looked at me, unseeing, with heavy bloodshot eyes.

Over a few drinks he poured out his tale of woe. There were no longer as many punters in the West End. The four hundred pounds a day that he used to earn trickled down to thirty or forty. He spent almost every penny on the horses or cheap bottles of whisky. His speech was slurred, and every so often he stopped mid-sentence to just sit and stare. Half the things he said didn't make any sense. He smelt like he hadn't washed for days. He must have had some kind of breakdown. When I first met him all those years ago he was so carefree.

I couldn't leave him like that. He always put me up when I needed to lie low for a bit, so I took him back to my flat. He kept talking about his kids and his ex-wife. I didn't even know he'd been married. He stayed with me for a few days. I even went with him to see a psychiatrist.

She confirmed that he'd had a breakdown. Alcohol, crime and prison had all taken their toll. I think the thing that sent him over the edge was the fact that his kids wanted nothing to do with him. I found that strange because the Stan I met all those years ago wouldn't have cared about that. As long as he was making enough money for his bets and his booze he was happy. Now drink just seemed to make him more miserable.

I was relieved when he left my flat. I prided myself on not being scared of anything, but seeing what he'd turned into gnawed at the edges of my own invincibility. I gave him a few hundred quid and told him to let me know if he needed anything.

I still accepted armed jobs every so often. The contacts I'd made over the years through gambling dens and my time inside, as well as my reputation, meant that I was never short of offers for that kind of work. Usually there was a phone call a couple of days before.

'Steve, I've got a job you might be interested in.'

'Yeah?'

'It's this Wednesday. There's a lorry leaving the depot. It'll be full of high-quality leather coats. I've got a buyer: he's willing to pay fifty grand. I've got Jim driving and a guy with a van for the exchange. The lorry will be coming out of the gates at 8:30 in the morning. Do you want it?'

'Yeah, go on, I'll have some of that.'

Wednesday morning I was on the pavement round the corner from the depot. Jim was across the street. The lorry came out at 8:30. A van pulled out in front of the lorry and stopped.

I walked up to the window. 'Excuse me mate, you wouldn't know where . . .' That was enough to get his attention and I opened the door, put a gun to his head and made him move over.

I sat down next to him with my arm round his shoulder and my gun pressed into his side. Jim jumped in and drove the lorry. We drove a few streets away and then stopped. I took the driver into the back of the lorry, tied him up and told him to shut up. I sat there with him, holding the gun, just in case he tried anything. We drove further on. The van did the exchange and that was it.

Without fear, any crime is possible. When I put a gun to somebody's head, I always saw the fear in their eyes. The victims looked into mine and saw I was there to do a day's work. They knew that I would pull the trigger or cut their throat if I had to. I wasn't going to leave without what I'd come for. Some tried to be brave, but I quickly took that under control. I tied them up, or put handcuffs on them. Sometimes I had to hold a knife to their throat to make them shut up. Sometimes, many times, they cried. They didn't know whether they were going to live or die, whether they would ever see their wife or kids again. I had no feelings towards them. Why would I? If I had feelings I wouldn't have been doing this; I'd have been out doing an honest day's work. I've never been a victim of crime.

I stayed out of prison for a couple of years. The sentences attached to gun-crime were longer than those for burglary – maybe I was more careful. It had been nearly two years since I found Stan slumped at the bar when I was checking out some flats for possible jobs near where he lived. The pub was quiet, and a few almost familiar faces turned to watch me walk in. Stan's usual seat was empty. I bought myself a pint and rolled a cigarette. They hadn't changed the wallpaper in that place in years. It was yellowed with smoke. I waited a few minutes in case he was in the toilets. I recognised the barman. He was drying some pint glasses.

''Scuse me, mate. Have you seen Stan? I don't know if he's still a regular here. You know who I mean, though? Dark hair. Normally sits in that corner over there.'

He looked at me, nodding slowly. Then he put down the glass he was drying. 'Sorry. I thought you'd have known. Stan died about eighteen months ago.'

'Died?'

'Something to do with his liver I think. You know how much he drank.'

'Yeah, I know. Was there a funeral?

'I suppose there must have been, but I don't think anyone from here went.'

'What happened? Was anyone with him when he died?'

'He hadn't come in for a few days, which was unusual for him. I heard one of his neighbours found him in his flat. He'd been dead a few days.'

Stan. Dead. He was fifty-seven. To most people he was just another alcoholic drowning himself in a bottle. 'Good riddance,' some people might have even thought. But this was Stan. Stan the charmer, the gambler, the con man. Stan, who always gave me a place to stay when I was in trouble. Everyone in my life either died or left me – my mum, Gary, Sue, Roz, George, Veronica, little Charlotte, and now Stan. Who was left? I threw myself with renewed vigour into the only thing I knew. Crime.

I met up with Paul again – the first time I saw him outside prison. He looked like a different person, he was gaunt and skinny with his eyes in the back of his head. He must have weighed eight stone. When he was inside he hadn't had access to the quantity of drugs and once he was out he lost control. His heroin habit was costing him nearly a thousand pounds a day. My lifestyle was expensive, too. We always got on well – I probably trusted him as much as I trusted anyone – so it made sense to start working together.

One day we went out and ripped a telephone box from a wall. We took it home to see if we could work out how it opened. Once we understood the mechanism, we could open any phone box quickly and neatly – no need to rip it off the wall. It was quick, easy money. The whole process – opening it, emptying it and leaving it locked back up again – took just two minutes. One evening we went down one side of Oxford Street and up the other robbing the phone boxes. In forty-five minutes we got four and a half grand. We could travel the country and make three or four thousand pounds a day. It was quite organised: we stayed in hotels, financing the trip as we went along. We always came back with quite a bit of money. I spent my money on women, clothes, holidays, cars, jewellery, gambling and occasionally drugs. Paul spent all of his on heroin.

That came to an end when they reinforced the doors on the phone boxes – although we were having disagreements by then anyway. Paul's addiction had a limit: once he had enough money for his heroin, he wanted to stop. I wouldn't give up until there was nowhere left to rob, or I got caught. Paul accused me of pushing my luck, but I couldn't stop while I knew there were phone boxes and easy houses that I hadn't robbed yet. He stole for drugs; stealing was my drug. Our working relationship fizzled out.

It was coming up to Christmas, which is a good time to burgle because people tend to keep more cash at home as well as expensive presents. The night I met Natalie I'd checked out several properties for the next day and decided to go for a drink.

She was tiny; she almost looked too young to be in a pub, and she was from a totally different world. I watched her for a while as she talked and laughed with her friends. There was something beautiful in her eyes, something I barely knew. Innocence. I wanted her. I could be good at small talk when I wanted to be. I bought her a drink knowing she could see how thick with notes my wallet was. She laughed and flirted. She was easy to charm.

'So what is it you do for a living then, Steve?'

'I'm a mini-cab driver, darlin'. I do a bit of this an' a bit of that.'

We saw each other at the pub again on New Year's Eve. I bought her drinks and told her how beautiful she was, how intelligent, how I'd never met anyone like her and how I wasn't sure I could live without her. I needed her, I told her. I knew by instinct that she needed to be needed. She looked up at me and fell for it all. She fell in love with me. She invited me to a family wedding a week later and introduced me to her parents. They didn't like the fact that I was thirty-three while their daughter was just twenty, but I charmed them too. I paid her mum compliments and asked her dad's opinions. I made sure they saw how attentive I was to their daughter. Before long I moved into her flat.

Once I was living with her, it became difficult to hide my criminal life. She should have left me once she found out but, like all the other women in my life, she thought she could change me. She was just part of it all, a good-looking girl on my arm. I drew her into the cycle. Drug dealers and armed robbers started visiting the flat. We put up people who were on the run from prison or the police, people who'd skipped bail. These were the people I respected. These were my associates. I considered them normal people. Lying low from the police, stashing money, drugs, guns – it was all just part of the life I lived. The people I couldn't understand were those who went

to work every day and came home with a pittance every
week.

I came home very late one night after a job. The light
was on and I could see Natalie's face at the window,
waiting. She should have been in bed asleep. When I
came through the door she turned to me, still waiting.
What was I seeing in her face? Fear? Pain? Desperation?
I could hear the clock ticking in the kitchen and Natalie
breathing. Her breath had misted the window where
she'd been watching for me. I started to feel angry that
she was awake. She should have been asleep so she
didn't know what time I came through the door, or what
time I eased myself into the bed next to her. If she'd just
gone to bed there'd be no condemning silences daring to
be broken.

'What are you doing up at this time Nat?'

More silence. The clock kept ticking.

'I'm pregnant, Steve.'

I still couldn't read her face. The words made sense,
but nothing else about the way she was looking at me
did. I hesitated.

'That's great news. Isn't it? What are you looking so
miserable for?'

She didn't say anything for a long time. Her lip was
trembling and she didn't look at me. A police siren rup-
tured the silence. I tensed up. I felt the rush in my stomach. My eyes flicked towards the back door. I couldn't
help it. The siren faded.

Natalie started sobbing.

'What is it Nat? Nat? Don't cry.'

'What kind of life can we give this baby? What . . .'
She put her hands over her face and rocked herself. I
could see tiny splashes where her tears hit the floor.

'Don't worry about that. Honestly Nat, I'll go straight.
Don't cry. I'll get a proper job and you won't have to

worry about anything. There's nothing to cry about. We'll be a proper little family. Promise.'

She got up and put her hand in mine, just like a child, and led me to bed.

As if I could go straight. If anything I needed to steal more with a baby on the way. At least that's what I told myself. I started coming home earlier so Natalie wouldn't worry. I took her on holiday to the Canaries for a fortnight. She needed the break, as the pregnancy was making her tired. I also needed to lie low for a bit after some jobs, although she didn't know that. It was a good two weeks. I even tried not to burgle while we were there. On the flight home I watched her sleep. She looked the happiest I'd seen her in ages, with her hand resting protectively on her bump. The worry creases that played on her forehead had relaxed and her often pale face looked radiant from the sun. I put my hand over hers and she woke. She looked up at me in a way she hadn't for a long time, like she trusted me. She held my hand as we walked into Heathrow airport.

The police were there, waiting for me. I was arrested for eight counts of burglary. I could have been famous, with all those people staring at me as I was cuffed and read my rights. As they led me out of the airport towards a waiting police car, I glanced back. Natalie was still standing there, a tiny pregnant figure, surrounded by suitcases and looking completely alone.

I saw Natalie for twenty minutes at the police station. I didn't ask her how she'd got home from the airport. She looked stunned and sick, like my mum looked the first time she came to the police station for me. The stab of guilt I felt when I saw her only made me angry. I was stealing for her. How else did she suppose I'd be able to afford the pushchair she wanted and all those baby clothes? Although I'd gambled away more than half of the burglary money she didn't know that. She couldn't look me in the eyes. I thought she might be sick. She had that look on her face like she'd had in the first few weeks of pregnancy, when she'd rush to the bathroom without warning and I'd hear her retching her guts up. She just sat opposite me staring at her hands, not really saying anything. It made me uncomfortable. I reassured her everything would be all right. I'd said it all before. I knew it probably wouldn't be the last time. I needed somewhere to go if I got bail. I needed her.

'I'm sorry, Nat. I know now I need to change. Stand by me Nat and I promise I'll change. I'll do it for you. I love you Nat. Promise.'

She still didn't speak. She just looked at me, broken, and I knew she'd do what I wanted. I was bailed two days later.

She brought her parents with her to court for my sentencing. She looked even paler – all traces of our holiday five months earlier were completely gone. As far as my in-laws were concerned, my charm had completely worn off. We now had an eight-week-old baby boy, Robbie. I was glad Natalie was there. Judges tend to give more lenient punishments if there's a wife and baby to look after. I got a suspended sentence.

Natalie was nearly always up when I got home, however late it was. She didn't accuse me or ask me where I'd been – although I avoided looking into her eyes. It was bad enough when she cried, but more and more I saw that bleak look in her face I'd seen for the first time at the airport. When I came home she put her arms round my neck and pressed her fragile body to me, relieved I was spending the night at home rather than in a cell.

Natalie fell pregnant again and we had a little girl, Terrie. I knew she was still hoping I'd change, but I didn't want to any more. I was who I was, and no woman or child was going to force me to be anything else. Natalie looked after the children while their daddy went out to 'work.' She still waited up into the night for me to come home, but each time her eyes betrayed more anger and more pain. She was only staying with me for the kids.

10

It's six a.m. The bathroom light is whirring and it's getting on my nerves. I finish shaving, smooth down my hair, and peer in the mirror. Do I look old? Nah, must be that damn light. I consider smashing it, but I don't want trouble with the hotel. It's still dark outside.

This time yesterday, I was home. I got dressed and packed my things quietly so I didn't wake up Natalie or the kids. I hated it when they asked me about my work. I even hated to look at them before I went on a job, because I was never sure if I was coming home that night – or four years later. I pulled the door shut gently and headed towards my car. It was a new one. Silver. I was dressed like a businessman on his way to work. First stop was Hackney to pick up the girls. They were waiting for me. They had their four grams of brown to see them through the day at least. If they needed any more I'd have to get it for them – they couldn't work without it. It was a long drive to Portsmouth. The stench of them burning their gear was getting up my nose. I opened the window, but they moaned that it made the lighter go out. When they finished they slept for fifteen minutes and then did it again – stinking the car out all the way to Portsmouth. I thought how amazing it was I never got addicted after ten years of inhaling it. I tried to ignore them and thought about the jobs we were going to do. Once I booked us into the hotel I'd leave the girls there and pick out some properties for tomorrow. I gripped the steering wheel tighter and floored the accelerator. It promised to be a good couple of days.

'Police! Police! Stay where you are. This is the police.'

It couldn't have been worse. I was on remand awaiting sentence and I was looking at four years.

Natalie brought the kids to visit me inside. I sat waiting for them outside the visiting room with all the other cons, wondering what my family would make of the high walls topped with double coils of razor wire. How would they cope with being searched by the screws? Natalie told the kids this was where their daddy worked, building and painting the walls and, because it was a long way away, I had to sleep there. Terrie might have been convinced, she was only four, but Robbie was six. He knew something wasn't right.

Little Terrie was crying by the time she got to the table because the screws had made her take out her hair band, to make sure she wasn't smuggling anything in her ponytail.

We had an hour to talk but it was hard to know what to say – sitting on plastic chairs surrounded by other prisoners and visitors on plastic chairs, all trying to manage their own desperate lives. The screws didn't like prisoners having any physical contact with visitors and they scrutinised and suspected every move. I wasn't going to give them any reason to come over and upset my family, so I avoided all contact.

I could tell Nat was exhausted from the four and a half hour train journey with the kids – and from lying to them that everything was normal. Once Terrie stopped crying she sat swinging her legs on the chair, staring round the room at everyone and everything. She seemed fascinated by it all. Every so often she asked Natalie a question.

'Why does Daddy have the blue chair and we had the red ones?'

'Why did that man at the desk make me take out my ponytail? Didn't he like my ponytail? I wanted Daddy to see my ponytail!'

'Why does Daddy have the same clothes as all the other men?'

'Mummy, when's Daddy coming home?'

Robbie just looked scared. It was almost a relief when the hour was up, although the goodbye was pretty uncomfortable. I'd spent my entire life detaching myself from everyone, so when Robbie screamed and kicked and clung on to my legs and refused to let go, I didn't feel emotion other than exasperation. But I could see something in Natalie's face as she tore him off. I was pretty good at reading people, but I wasn't sure what I saw that day. I decided she was just tired. I had to stay focused.

The police kept hassling me while I awaited sentencing – probably because they didn't have enough evidence to put me away for as long as they wanted. I'd been burgling that area for five years; I certainly wasn't going to do them any favours.

'Perhaps, Cattell, if you are unable to cooperate, we should pay your wife a visit and see what she has to say.'

'Do what you like. She doesn't know anything.'

I never really thought they would, until my solicitor visited me and told me Natalie had had a visit from the police. They knocked on the door at six in the morning and took her away for questioning. They asked her about me for four hours and locked her in a cell. Natalie had never been involved in any of my criminal activities and she was traumatised. She'd only seen the visiting room of a prison before. I couldn't understand what was going on. She was bailed to go back to the police station three weeks later.

When I had my phone call later that week, Natalie answered as normal until she knew it was me, then she started crying.

'What is it Nat? What's happened?'

'They arrested me.'

'Yeah, I know – on Monday.'

'They came back, Steve.'

'They what?'

'They came round yesterday and arrested me for conspiracy. Steve, I don't even know what conspiracy is. They took me to the station in the police car. The kids were screaming. They were really scared. I was really scared.'

'Did you tell them anything?'

'I was hiding in the kitchen with the children. The police were banging and shouting through the letterbox saying if I didn't open the door they would smash it in. It was horrible. I didn't know what to do.'

'But did you tell them anything?'

'Like what, Steve?'

'Don't worry, I'm sure you did fine.'

'Did fine? I've been taken away from my kids and questioned for twelve hours.'

'I just meant . . .'

'I know what you meant. Just so you know, I've been bailed to appear in six weeks' time.'

She hung up. It was unlike her, but I suppose she was shaken. I'd borrowed her car for a job in Hampshire and got a speeding ticket, which she'd signed and paid for. When she was questioned she told the truth: that she'd never been to Hampshire. She was charged with conspiracy to pervert the course of justice. That's a crown court offence. She collapsed on the way out of the station and had to be sedated. I blamed the police. I knew they were just using her to try to get to me, but there was no way I was going to give them the satisfaction of a confession.

I stood in the dock with my criminal associates on one side of me and my wife on the other. The judge threw her case out due to lack of evidence; I got three years and nine months.

Initially I was sent to Winchester prison. It was 1997. The prison system had just been computerised and the old files had been destroyed. Nobody knew my history and I went in as a new prisoner. As a result, I ended up being transferred to Ford open prison.

I'd never been to an open prison before. I couldn't believe my luck. I would choose four weeks at Ford open prison over four weeks in Butlins any day. It was amazing – like a holiday camp. We could go through the forest to Tescos and buy a bottle of Scotch, we could get drugs on tap, there were four or five full-size snooker tables and a cinema that seated two hundred with different films on every night. We could play table tennis, cricket and mini-golf. The food was five-star. There were no locks, no bars and I never saw a prison officer. A sentence there would certainly be no deterrent for anybody to stop their criminal lifestyle. I can't understand why they exist. Open prisons serve no purpose whatsoever, except maybe to get someone used to the outside world after a long sentence of isolation.

We could have two days leave every month. Most people booked a hotel by the seaside in Littlehampton and invited their wife or girlfriend down, went to the pub for a few pints, then spent the day in bed. I'd been there two months when I got my first day release. I went to Littlehampton seaside too, but I didn't invite Natalie. I walked along the promenade searching for potential burglaries to do on my release. Some of the guesthouses and holiday homes would be easy money. The rest of day I spent at the betting shop with the little money I had.

When I returned to the prison I began to wonder if I had some kind of problem. I would rather plan crimes for my release than see the family I'd been separated from. My sole objective of day release was planning burglaries. I was more like Paul and the other heroin addicts I knew than I'd realised – except heroin wasn't my drug.

I got fed up with open prison – sunbathing all day, eating and playing cricket got boring. So I absconded. It wasn't difficult – I just walked as far as the prison boundary and kept going. I slept under some stairs the first night. The next day I stole some equipment from Woolworth's for three burglaries. The money from those enabled me to buy some new clothes, book into a hotel, refresh myself and prepare to get back into my lifestyle. I organised to pick up a car from someone I'd met in the prison. What I didn't know was that he was a grass and, as I arrived to meet him, I was apprehended by the police. I was transferred to a closed prison to finish my sentence.

I used to write to Natalie, telling her I loved her and promising her that I would give up crime and put my family first. I suppose I believed it while I was writing. I used to sit at the small table under the window in my cell where the light was best. I could see an

Unbreakable

old-fashioned detached house with bay windows through the bars, probably four hundred metres away from the prison grounds. I gazed out of the window for hours. Each weekday morning at 7:40 a man dressed in a suit got into his BMW and drove down the road. He never returned before six in the evening. An hour later a woman struggled through the front door with a buggy and a dog straining at its lead. She walked in the direction of the recreation ground and wasn't back for an hour. I knew how easy those old bay windows were to open. If I waited until she was out of sight, I'd have at least forty minutes undisturbed in that house. It amused me that they'd probably bought that dog as a guard dog and, when I turned up with my crowbar and bag to fill, it wouldn't be there to bark.

I looked back down at the letter I was writing. I suppose I should have felt guilty making those promises I didn't intend to keep. I shouldn't have sent it. But I did. Generally Natalie seemed to be coping with me being inside. But sometimes, especially after she received these letters, she was more open during our phone calls. I didn't always like it. She told me how money was tight and that the kids kept having nightmares. She told me Robbie was struggling at school and wasn't eating properly, and Terrie was wetting herself. I decided not to write so many of those letters. I preferred it when Natalie was coping.

Natalie and I broke up while I was inside. She finally realised, I think, that she couldn't change me and she wasn't prepared to let herself or the kids suffer any more. It irritated me because it meant I had to arrange somewhere else to live on my release. Before the sentence, I'd been having an affair – just another piece of my lifestyle. An affair provided back-up in case my wife left me when I ended up back in prison. It was someone else to visit me, someone else to put me up. When I got out this time it was necessary. Natalie wasn't willing, so I persuaded this old girlfriend to give me somewhere to stay.

It took me four weeks to charm my way back into Natalie's life, and the house. My promise was always the same – it's over, I've changed, I will be a dad and a husband. To prove to Natalie that I was willing to change, I even agreed to move away. It would be a fresh start, I told her, away from my old haunts and my old associates.

After three days in Northampton I was burgling again. Did anybody really think that putting me in a new place would change the person I had become? Nothing was going to change me now – not even our third child, Lillie, who was born in our new home. Robbie and Terrie had grown up so much while I was inside. I missed out on three years of their lives. At first I liked them following me everywhere when I was at home. But it quickly became a nuisance – they made such a fuss whenever I went out. Natalie explained they were scared that if I went out I might not come back.

I went to do some jobs in Littlehampton that I'd picked out during my day release at Ford open prison. I was walking along the promenade when I bumped into Paul. He was there with another heroin addict breaking into phone boxes. I told him to book into the hotel I was staying in, which he did. As we walked upstairs I pulled two room keys from my pocket.

'Who are you with then, Steve?'

'I'm not with anyone.'

'How come you've got two rooms then?'

'Come and have a look.'

I opened the door to reveal a hotel room totally packed with electrical equipment. Paul was gob-smacked.

'Look at all this stuff! What are you still doing here? You may as well go back. You must have got enough by now?'

'Nah, I've got hours yet.'

'You're crazy, Steve. You haven't changed a bit.'

We had a few pints together and chatted about our phone box days. Paul lived in Northampton with his girl-friend, Maxine. We arranged to meet up there a week later. It didn't take long for us to find a way we could work together: drugs. Paul was an addict, so there was no way he could sell heroin himself – he'd have used it all. He told me he'd had a scare a couple of weeks before: he'd overdosed on heroin and almost died. I occasion-ally used crack cocaine, but I wasn't addicted so I wouldn't be tempted to use the drugs. Paul had connec-tions to an extensive network of people in the heroin world. If I dispensed the drugs and Paul provided the customers, we could work together and split the profits. We rented a house in Northampton which became a drug den.

I remember serving up a bag of brown to a fifteen-year-old girl – the same age Charlotte had been when she died. This girl shot it up in her arm right in front of me. I watched her start shaking and opening and closing her mouth. She began to turn blue. Even her lips were turning blue. She'd overdosed and I nearly panicked. I didn't give a crap about her. It wasn't about her – it was about getting the manslaughter charge and going to prison. That would mean an end to the burgling. As a human being she meant nothing to me. As a prison sentence she meant an awful lot. Fortunately she came back, coughing and crying and vomiting all over the floor.

Was I evil? I don't believe anyone is born evil, but kids on the streets are vulnerable to an evil lifestyle. Eventually, I know, I had no regard for human life. The only life I cared about was my own life of crime and it controlled me. My passion was to have power over other people, to do what I wanted when I wanted. When I'd get caught and was spending twenty-three hours a day incarcerated in a cell, mostly in solitary confinement, just getting through each day was a struggle. Only hate and anger got me through. The streets were my life; crime was my life. There were times I'd be able to go into a pub and get drunk every night for a month without paying for a single drink because people 'respected' me.

Everyone I knew was a criminal. I was living in a family of crime. I could call on anybody to do anything I wanted. I could call on somebody to kill someone, for a price or a favour. I could call on somebody to deliver drugs for me. I could call on somebody to travel from a couple of hundred miles away to come and pick up a room full of stolen stuff. I could call on anybody to do anything – even to do my weekly shopping on cheque fraud. I could call on somebody to stop the electric meter going round so I saved on my electric bill. I could get a bent MOT. I could get driving licences and passports made up. I could become anyone I wanted to be. I could change my appearance. That's the cycle of crime. That's the adrenaline buzz.

Selling heroin is easy money when you have no conscience. Oddly, I was still living mostly off the proceeds of burglaries – that's what most of my clients did to get money to buy drugs. The drug den was separate from the house with Natalie and the kids. It was the best of both worlds: I was husband and father when it suited me, heroin dealer when it didn't. Paul and I got on well, better than we had before when Paul wanted to stop once he had enough for his fix. It was a steady income and Paul didn't have to worry about running out of heroin. It was going well until the heroin house in Northampton was raided.

Paul had gone out. I was sitting behind the desk texting Natalie that I was at a lock-in in the pub and would be home soon. The house was quiet except for the breathing of one satisfied customer slumped in the corner, his hand curled around his syringe. There were no sirens, no warning. The front door hadn't been shut properly. I looked up from my phone to see two police officers in the doorway. The desk I was sitting at contained money, scales and more brown than Paul would use in a year. I was arrested for possession with intent to supply. I wasn't about to grass up Paul, so it was just me.

Since it was the first drug offence I'd ever had, I made bail with fixed address: Natalie. Three days after I was bailed I was back into a cycle of burglary again. I knew if I got caught while on bail for the drug offences I'd get put away for a long time, but I just couldn't help myself. As part of an assessment before I received my sentence I was sent to see a criminal psychologist. He helped me to understand that I had an addiction to crime. A lot of my friends were drug addicts. I'd seen Paul going through heroin withdrawal: getting anxious and throwing up. I used to think how pathetic it was to be controlled by drugs. I hadn't realised that I was just the same.

11

A couple of months after I was bailed, I had a phone call from Paul.

'Steve?'

'Yeah?'

'I think I've got a job for us. You still up for it?'

'What do you think?' I asked him.

'Well, I just thought, what with the intent to supply charge, you might be keeping your head down.'

'If I'm going to prison, I'm going to prison. It's practically home anyway. What's the job?

'I'm at this faith camp in Peterborough.'

'Faith camp?'

'It's this camp for Christians. My mate Mark's been bugging me for ages to go. I told him I'm not interested in all his Christian stuff and to leave me alone. Anyway, to cut a long story short, I had this massive bust up with Maxine and ended up walking out of the house with the raging hump, only to find Mark outside with his van and a spare ticket to this camp. I had enough gear on me to see me through the week so I said I'd go. Anyway mate, now I'm here, I reckon we could make loads. There's a meeting in a big marquee every night and everyone leaves their tents and all their stuff for about an hour.'

'Sounds easy. All we'd need is a Stanley knife. We could cut open hundreds of tents in an hour. Stay one night and see what you think, and call me tomorrow with what time to come, OK?'

'OK, see you Steve.'

I waited, but the phone call never came. It got to Thursday – still nothing. I started to get annoyed with Paul – typical heroin addict. I just knew he nicked everything for himself. That's what heroin addicts do – they're very selfish people. They don't even look after their friends in crime. The more I thought about it, the angrier I got, so once the week was up I steamed round to his house in Northampton and hammered on the door. Seeing him smile at me on the doorstep really wound me up.

'Thanks a lot, mate. You're a nice friend you are. There must have been thousands of cheque books and credit cards at that camp. More than you'd know what to do with. I can't believe you kept it all for yourself.'

'No Steve. That's not how it happened. You've got to listen to this.'

'I should have grassed you up about the drugs.'

'Please Steve.'

He looked different. I couldn't say how. He wasn't quite as skinny, I think. His eyes were more focused, maybe, and he had energy – not the nervous energy of a heroin addict starting withdrawal either. It was hard to say exactly what it was. I walked past him into the house and sat at the little table in the kitchen.

'Well come on then. Spit it out.'

Paul went to the fridge, got out a beer and handed it to me. He didn't sit down.

'That night I rang you from the camp, I went to the evening meeting with Mark. I hated it. Everyone was singing and putting their hands in the air. You know my habit's been bad recently? I was injecting heroin three times a day, and even I thought these people were nuts.

So I said to Mark, I'll stay and camp but I'm not going to any more of these meetings. I don't like them. All this God stuff is not for me. Mark couldn't really argue so we left it at that. Anyway a bit later in the week Mark and his wife reckoned they'd been praying and God had told them to tell me to come to the meeting.'

'And you went? I don't believe I'm hearing this. You were supposed to be ringing me so I could come up and we could make lots of money.'

'Gimme a chance, mate. I went to keep the peace. The meetings were only about an hour, Mark was bugging me, so I went. There was this black guy preaching. Wilfred Lyle his name was. He said that the Holy Spirit had spoken to him and told him there were people in the place who were struggling with drugs and he wanted them to come forward now and God was going to release them. Of course Mark starts nudging me but there's no way I'm going to go to the front. Some people had already gone up but then this speaker starts shouting that there's someone in this place who needs to be released from heroin, and I think, well, I've been through two rehabs – I've nearly died from overdosing. So maybe it was worth a try. I got up and made my way towards the front.

'There was a long line of people already there waiting to be prayed for and the speaker was miles away, so I just shut my eyes and said in my head, 'If you're real God, help me, please help me!' and then I opened my eyes and this black preacher is standing right in front of me. He put his hands on my head and prayed for me. It was weird, I walked out of there feeling different, like something had changed, you know what I mean? And I went back to my little one-man tent for a fag before bed. I had a little candle in there, because my torch had run out of batteries, and I just sat for a while in my sleeping bag wondering what was going on.

'I was feeling different but I didn't quite know how. I knew something had changed but I didn't know what. I had no idea about this God stuff so I thought, 'I'm not going to understand what's going on tonight so I'll sleep on it.' I blew out the candle and suddenly I was surrounded by light. It was quite scary, but it was like, without anyone explaining it, I kind of understood a lot of stuff – like I'd always known it somehow. And I kept feeling emotions and I felt like someone was saying there was a chance for me. All I had to do was stop sinning and get baptised and I would be met at baptism where everything would be confirmed. And then it just stopped and it went dark again. I was soaked through with sweat. I was so frightened. I legged it out of my tent but everyone else was in bed 'cos of the curfew, so I couldn't talk to anyone 'til morning. I thought I might have gone mad – totally lost the plot. I just walked around the campsite all night. I didn't dare go back to my tent in case whatever it was was still there. I wondered if it was some kind of heroin flashback. I just didn't know and then I remembered that I had to get baptised and then everything would be confirmed. I didn't even really know what baptism was.

'As soon as Mark's pastor came out of his tent the next morning I was there waiting. I told him what happened and he kind of looked at me strange, you know, and I told him I needed to get baptised. He said we'd better wait 'til we get back to church but I wasn't having that – I need to get baptised that day, immediately. He wasn't sure so I got angry and said there are hundreds of pastors here and if he didn't want to do it then I'd find one who would. I was desperate to know what was happening to me because, if nothing happened at baptism, I'd know that what I'd experienced was a lie – I'd invented it. And I was so sure it was real.

'So we found this river and Mark and the pastor went in with me and quite a few people came to watch and, standing there in the water, it just seemed so ridiculous. I felt like I was in shock. I thought I'd definitely gone mad and was just about to say so and try and get out of this baptism thing when this warmth flooded through me. It went up through my body and through my head – a loving warmth, a really powerful passionate feeling. There were like waves of it. And it was so powerful and physical it made me cry out. They baptised me and the power of whatever it was that was on me knocked them both over and I had to grab them both and pull them out of the water. Mark's been a Christian eight years and he said he'd never felt the power of God like that before. I just knew God had to be real. I don't know the ins and outs of the Bible – just that God is real. I've come off heroin. You know I've done rehabs, but I've always gone back. I asked God to take the desire away and he has. Everything's changed.'

Paul looked at me, expectantly.

'You're nuts,' I said and took a long swig of my beer.

Paul started phoning me up regularly after his conversion. He was so passionate about this God, just as he used to be passionate about heroin. He stayed clean for a record length of time. He continued to put on weight and Maxine hadn't thrown him out again since the camp. They were even planning to get married. My phone conversations with him always followed the same pattern.

'God's spoken to me,' Paul would say. 'All you've got to do is change your plea and accept Jesus into your life.'

'You are seriously nuts, mate. You back on the drugs or something?'

'What I'm telling you is true, Steve. Jesus is the only one who can help you.'

'Paul, do us a favour? Go away and leave me alone.'

'You've got to give your life to Christ. I'm telling you – that's the only way.'

'The way I see it, I've got two options: get a lot of money and do a runner before my sentencing; or get a lot of money and put it to one side. That way, when I get out, I can carry on the lifestyle that I've got – I'll have something to look forward to while I serve my time.'

It was easy for him to tell me to change my plea to guilty. He'd got away with it. I had to accept that I had a sentence coming – maybe my longest yet – and I had to prepare myself for it. That meant closing all the doors, lying my way into a reduced sentence, using all the mitigation I could. I was pleased that Paul had kicked the heroin addiction, but all the God talk was a bit much. Although I made it clear I thought it was a load of rubbish, he kept on phoning me. Part of me was glad he called me because he was still my mate. And even I couldn't deny the massive change in him. Part of me felt gutted, though. Everything in Paul's life seemed to be working out for him. Being on bail was really getting me down. I think I was waiting for the call from Maxine, or the lapse of contact that would tell me Paul had gone back to his drugs. But Maxine never called and Paul never stopped calling.

But eventually Paul's calls began to wear me down. He seemed so sure that holding my hands up to everything would protect me from prison, but it made no logical sense. I asked my barrister.

'What would happen,' I said, almost embarrassed to ask, 'if I pleaded guilty to the drugs charge?'

He looked at me from across his desk and raised his eyebrows. 'At best, Steve, you'd be looking at four years in prison.'

I nodded. What else could I expect?

'Our best option,' he said, 'is to make a case for mitigating circumstances and to plead not guilty.'

'Right, OK,' I said. 'You're probably right, but I'll have a think and let you know what I decide.'

We shook hands and I left. I took the long way home, mulling over the different angles of the situation. In all these years caught in the cycle of crime and punishment I'd never given a second thought to my plea. I decided to go with the barrister. He had to know better than a recovering smack-head.

I continued to burgle almost every day I was on bail. I began to think of myself as a junkie to the crime habit. I'd just arrived back home after a couple of days away doing several jobs. Natalie had gone out with the girls and I was watching cartoons with Robbie when the police arrived.

'It's the police! Open up!'

Robbie looked up at me – I recognised that look from the day he'd clung to me in the prison visiting room and wouldn't let go. He ran to hide behind the settee.

'Open up!' They were shouting and banging on the door. 'Police! We're coming in!'

'Dad!' Robbie whispered fiercely.

'It's okay, don't worry.' I remained seated, refusing to open the door.

They smashed through the door.

'Go next door!' I shouted to Robbie. 'And wait there 'til Mum comes home.'

He hesitated and I saw that look again.

'Well, go on then.'

He shot past us and into the neighbour's house as the police slapped on the cuffs and bundled me into the car outside. Curtains were twitching.

As I sat in the interview room waiting for my solicitor to arrive from London I wondered how Natalie would react. Even I was getting bored with the lies – the empty promises I heard myself making. I decided not to ring her until I had to.

I decided I would conduct a 'no comment' interview. The police were paid to catch me. I wasn't paid to grass myself up, so why should I do them any favours? I knew I was going into custody. Not only had I breached my bail conditions, but my record of previous convictions would ensure I spent time on remand before sentencing. I stared at the blank blue wall. My solicitor arrived and they started the tape rolling. I had the first 'no comment' ready to roll off my tongue. I still don't fully understand what happened next.

'Yeah,' I heard myself saying. 'I did all twelve burglaries you're charging me with. I can't help myself. I'm out of control. I can't walk past a house without burgling it, or coming back the next day with my tools if I can't do it there and then. When I'm not burgling houses I'm planning where to burgle next. And it's not just burgling – it's more serious crimes too. I can't wait to get out of prison so I can be out doing more. I'm defrauding banks, I'm defrauding building societies. I'm earning thirty thousand pounds a week. I'm doing six to eight thousand burglaries a year. I can't stop. I don't even want to be making this statement.'

'Can we stop this interview please? I want a word with my client.' My solicitor was looking at me like I'd gone mad.

They stopped the tape and he drew me aside. 'Listen to me, Steve. If you carry on like this, if you sign this statement, you're looking at the maximum of fourteen years, and they'll give it to you.'

'It doesn't matter,' I said. I picked up the pen. 'This has got to end. It has got to end today.'

I had no idea where this conviction came from. All I knew was that I couldn't stop myself.

My solicitor sighed. 'I'll see you in court in the morning,' he said. 'They'll remand you to Winchester tonight.'

'Can you ring my wife to bring in the usual – some money, clothes and my trainers?'

'Will do.' He hesitated a moment as he turned to leave. 'Take care of yourself, Steve.'

'Will do.'

He left and I put my head down on the table and closed my eyes. I tried to prepare myself for my night in the cells before my court appearance. I saw a long list of my crimes rolling in the darkness behind my eyelids: burglary, armed robbery, supplying heroin – and, underneath them all, my signature: S. Cattell. I heard the door open and shut, footsteps, a chair scraping. I pictured the cell where I'd be spending the night.

'Wakey wakey!'

I lifted my head and opened my eyes to see my property on the table in front of me.

'You're free to go, Mr Cattell. We're bailing you.'

My solicitor was standing in the doorway. He was shaking his head – he couldn't believe it. I couldn't believe it. I was on bail for the heroin charge. In the last forty-eight hours I'd committed twelve crimes and I'd just admitted that I couldn't stop committing crime. Each of those crimes could carry three years, but they were releasing me. It made no sense, but I didn't wait around to argue: I scooped up my things and went home.

On the way home from the police station I sensed something was wrong, but I couldn't put my finger on it at first. I sat staring out the window and suddenly I realised that, for the first time in decades, I wasn't looking at mortice locks on the houses I passed. The police station was already miles behind me and I hadn't identified any landmarks so I could find those houses again. I was just sitting there thinking about how I was bailed and going home and I wasn't planning burglaries for the coming week. I shook my head and sat back in my seat. I felt strange, different somehow. What was it? Was this freedom?

Natalie was sitting on the settee with the kids when I arrived home. I could tell she'd been crying. She looked like she'd seen a ghost when I came in.

'What are you doing here?'

'I . . . I don't know. They gave me bail. I pleaded guilty and they gave me bail.'

'Daddy's home!' The girls ran to me and nearly knocked me over. I saw something like a shadow of relief and a small smile pass over Robbie's face but he stayed where he was beside Natalie.

'That's great, Steve,' Natalie said quietly. She stood up and walked into the kitchen and I watched her go.

As soon as I could tear myself away from the girls I went into the bedroom to telephone Paul.

'You're never going to believe this, mate . . .' And I poured it all out, everything that had just happened. I hadn't strung that many words together in years. Paul just listened.

I was about halfway through my story when Natalie came in and sat on the bed beside me. She handed me a cup of tea. I smiled my thanks and continued talking to Paul.

'So,' I finished. 'I still can't believe they gave me bail. I told them everything, Paul, I told them I'm out of control and basically, when I get out, I'm gonna carry on burgling.'

I sensed Natalie stiffen beside me. She got up to leave.

On the other end of the phone I could almost hear Paul smiling. He may as well have said, 'I told you so.' Instead he said, 'You know what you've done? For the first time in your life you've opened your heart. You went into that police station and told the truth and the Lord has set you free.'

'I dunno about that, Paul. I think you'll find it was the chief inspector upstairs.'

'I know you don't get this Steve, but I've been praying for you and I know if you tell the truth, you'll go free.'

'Yeah? And I still think you're nuts.' I shook my head.

'You know what this means, Steve?'

'Don't start saying I should tell the truth about the drugs charges. This was a fluke, that's all. It's not as if I've got away with it either. I'll be banged up when I get sentenced in a few months anyway.'

'Is Paul excited that God got you bail?' Natalie was standing in the kitchen with her back to me when I walked in.

'Yeah, something like that.'

'Well God's got his work cut out for him.'

Even God didn't wipe away two outstanding court cases, though. I was out driving one day, about six weeks after I'd told the police the truth. Sometimes I did my best thinking while I was driving.

In those six weeks I hadn't committed a single crime. I was struggling with why I just didn't feel like it. What was wrong with me? How was I going to make a living?

I was also struggling under the weight of the two sentences hanging over me. I had two options: either to run and not appear, or to turn up and face the longest sentence I'd ever served. What should I do? What could I do?

Paul had rung again the day before.

'How are you doing, Steve?'

'I'm fine.'

'Have you been burgling?'

'No. Still nothing.'

'That's amazing, Steve. It really is.'

'Yeah. Look, Paul, I really don't want another lecture from you about God and what I should do with my life. Why don't you worry about your own life?'

'Steve, the last thing I want to do is lecture you. I'm only trying to help. It's just that my life has changed so completely. You know what I was like, Steve. You were there with me at the lowest point. Sometimes I still can't quite believe what's happened. I've gained four stone, and I can't even remember when I felt this healthy. Maxine and I are doing really well. I've got a job I actually like. I think I might be happy, Steve. For the first time in my life.'

'Yeah, well I'm really happy that you're happy mate. All this happiness. That's great.'

I felt bad when I hung up on him. I knew I was jealous. It must be nice to get away with it, not facing the rest of the foreseeable future in prison.

I pulled over to light a cigarette. Across the road was a church. I sat looking at it for a while, smoking. It was called St Paul's.

I looked at my watch. It was quarter to one. Natalie wouldn't be expecting me back for a while. I hadn't been inside a church since I was about seven. I finished my cigarette. Paul went to church every Sunday. I got out of the car and crossed the road. The door was big and heavy and shut. I tried the handle, not expecting it to move, but it opened easily. The place was deserted and I sat down near the back. The big stained glass window made blue and red gashes of light on the floor.

I was still thinking about how good Paul's life was. Mine was a mess. And where would we be, I wondered, if Paul had got caught with the heroin instead of me? I didn't know.

There was a wooden cross at the front of the church. I looked up at the ceiling, high above my head.

'If you're real God, why is it that you can change my friend Paul's life but you can't change mine?'

I sat in the silence for a while.

Nothing.

This was a waste of time. I walked out, got in my car and drove home.

12

Although I usually tried to visit Veronica a couple of times a week when I was out of prison, things had been so hectic since my last release I hadn't seen her in almost four years. After Charlotte died she'd moved out of the flat where I'd lived with them as a teenager and settled into a small London terrace with Elizabeth.

When I pulled up in front of the house I wasn't surprised to see that the tiny garden was full of used beer cans and broken glass and that one of the upstairs windows was boarded up. Veronica had never been particularly house-proud.

There was no answer when I knocked on the door. I tried again and waited around for a while, but no one came. I left and went back the next day – Veronica might have been out of it on drugs and unable to get to the door. But there was still no reply. By the third day I was getting worried and while I was banging on Veronica's door, the neighbour's door opened and an elderly woman came out.

'Who you lookin' for?'

'Veronica. D'you know her?'

'I did. But she don't live there no more. No one does.'

'Don't suppose you know where she is now?

'Nah, love. All I know is she ain't been there for months.'

I wondered if she'd gone back to the old flat. Elizabeth might have left home by now. The flat was only a twenty-minute walk away, so I left my car parked outside the terraces. It didn't look like the block had been repainted since I lived there. It used to be quite pleasant, but now it looked like a dump. I rang the bell. An old man answered. He didn't know a Veronica. I tried the bell on the other side of the hall where a young mum who was a friend of Veronica's used to live. Veronica would go and smoke a spliff with her, after a fight with George. She recognised me instantly.

'Steve. How are you? Good to see you out.'

'I'm fine. Cheers. Listen, I'm looking for Veronica. I went to the new house but she hasn't been there for a few days. Do you know where she is?'

I knew by the look on her face what she was going to say. I'd heard it too many times before.

'She's dead, Steve. I'm sorry. It was a couple of months ago. She got really into crack towards the end. And what with the drinking – you know – I guess she's with George now, yeah?'

I couldn't speak.

'I've got a number for Elizabeth. You want it?'

I nodded. My throat felt raw, like I'd just come out of months in the isolation unit. She handed me a scrap of paper with a number scribbled on it. I watched my hand reach out, take it and put it in the inside pocket of my jacket. I stared at her.

'Do you want to come in for a cup of tea or something?'

'Nah, you're all right.' I took a step back.

'You look after yourself then, Steve.' She shut the door.

I stood staring at the door covered with scratches and gouges and marks. It was painted prison-cell green.

Green supposedly stops people from going mad. I don't know how long I stood there, remembering Veronica and George and trying to take in that they were both dead. It was a long walk back to the car.

A few weeks later, Natalie came to me, exhausted.

'The kids have been at each other all day, Steve. My head is splitting and I need a break. Could you please take Lillie out for an hour?'

'Oh sure, no problem,' I agreed. 'Lillie and I'll have a great time, won't we?' I swung Lillie onto my shoulders and we were off. I had no idea what to do with an eighteen-month-old baby for an hour.

We went to the pub and I sat in the beer garden sipping my pint and staring at the river while she played in the sandpit. The sound of her screaming broke my reverie.

She was wailing and looking around frantically, tears streaming down her cheeks and blurring her vision. I realised she was screaming because she thought she'd lost me.

'Lillie! I'm right here!' I called and held out my arms to her.

As soon as she heard my voice, she saw me and started running as fast as her chubby little legs would take her. She stumbled, fell over, picked herself up, ran again, fell over, picked herself up and ran. When she finally fell into my arms she clung on as if she'd never let go. And as she hung on, something inside me began to soften.

I held on to her just as tightly. My stomach tensed. I reached up to wipe my eyes and discovered my cheeks were wet – I was crying. I held my baby and felt love, overwhelming emotion, everything a father should feel for his daughter.

And in that moment God answered the prayer I'd flung up in that church. It wasn't a dramatic conversion like the one Paul experienced, yet I knew something powerful was happening. In that moment I felt those unbreakable walls I had spent my life building to isolate me from the world begin to crumble. I felt vulnerable, but that didn't anger or frighten me. I walked home with Lillie in my arms and I relished these tender sensations. It was as though light was flooding into my soul. I don't know if I knew God, but I knew love, for the first time in my life I knew love, and it gave me a strangely familiar rush. I felt almost sick with this buzz – the only one that had ever matched the one I got from breaking into a house.

When I got home I found Natalie in the kitchen and I hugged her. I held her and held her. I never wanted to let go. I clung on to her like Robbie had clung on to me in the prison lounge, like Lillie had clung on to me when she found me. The tears flowed down my cheeks and I let them.

The next few weeks were an amazing time of discovery for this hardened criminal. I found out what it was to love and to be loved. Natalie had loved me for years, but I had never allowed myself to enjoy or accept it. I no longer had any desire to leave, to avoid the emotional responsibility that came with a family. I just wanted to be with them, with my family! I was home.

But with this amazing love came fear. I still had two court cases hanging over me, both certain to end in custodial sentences. Until now, prison had just been something to try to avoid. Now its prospect was terrifying. I had never loved my wife or my children, they had been a means to reduced sentences. Now they were everything.

I remembered a man I had met during my last prison sentence. We were playing table tennis with a tobacco bet that I was about to win (the score was nineteen-seventeen to me), when the gates opened for exercise.

When it's summer prisoners never waste an opportunity to go outside. After I made him agree to finish the game later, I went out while he went to make a phone call. Ten minutes later, the alarms went off. We were all brought inside and locked in the nearest cell. I could see yellow tape across a door at the other end of the corridor. It was the man I'd been playing table tennis with. His wife had told him she was leaving him and he'd gone to his cell, torn a strip from his sheet, and hanged himself. I was so annoyed I never got to beat him and collect my tobacco. It had seemed so stupid to me at the time – two wives had left me, but I didn't care. But when I thought about it now, it didn't seem stupid at all any more. In fact, his reaction made perfect sense to me.

The night before my court appearance for the burglaries, I went into the kids' bedrooms while they slept. I kissed Robbie and Terrie and Lillie gently and whispered goodbye. They didn't wake up. I couldn't bear to be separated from them any more. I wouldn't be.

I took eighty sleeping tablets to court with me the next morning. If I got sent down, I wasn't coming home again. I knew I could never get through prison now. I couldn't bear to watch my wife and children leaving after a visit every two weeks, knowing that might be the last time I'd see them. In prison, emotion is deadly – it can kill a man. I'd known too many people like my table tennis opponent who had cut their wrists or hanged themselves when their wives left them. Loving my wife changed everything. I didn't have the courage to slit my wrists or hang myself, so overdosing on sleeping tablets seemed an easier option. I'd just go to sleep and never have to wake up behind bars again.

Throughout this time, Paul had continued to phone me almost daily, and his words echoed in my head as I walked into court that day carrying my own death sentence.

'God's spoken to me, Steve,' he told me over and over again. 'You have to plead guilty. You've just got to tell the truth. Don't ask me how I know. Just tell the truth. Please.'

And my reply was the same every time. 'I don't think even God could get me out of this one, mate. So I'll send you a visiting order sometime. Come up and see us, yeah?'

The court case began. The prosecution threw everything at me: my previous convictions adding up to a total of twenty-four years in prison, the intent to supply class-A drugs charge, the statement I'd made admitting to being out of control. They even suggested I might have continued burgling while on bail and had just not been caught.

'By his own admission, your honour, Mr Cattell cannot walk past a house without burgling or planning to burgle it at a later date. He has admitted that he has no control over his actions. As soon as he is released he will continue to burgle. The only thing I can recommend in this case, your honour, is an extended custodial sentence.'

My barrister did his best, but there wasn't a lot he could say in my defence. I looked over at Natalie and wondered if it would be the last time I saw her. My head was pounding.

Finally the judge said, 'There will be a fifteen-minute adjournment, after which I will pass sentence.'

Everyone filed out of the courtroom. I sat on a bench in the waiting area outside and Natalie sat next to me. Each time I felt her squeeze my hand, I felt more and more desperate. There was nothing to say.

'We can't win today. You know that, don't you?' my barrister asked. He stood in front of us, arms folded and head tilted to one side. I wondered if he felt like a doctor who had to tell a patient they had only a few weeks to live.

'I know that. I'm not the same person that committed all those offences, but I'm going to prison today,' I almost whispered through gritted teeth. 'Everything the prosecution said is true. Everything's changed, I've changed, but how's the judge going to believe that with my record? I even confessed to being out of control – it's there in black and white. How could they not send me to prison today?'

I wondered if I'd feel any pain or if I'd just drift into sleep like any other night. I hoped Natalie could forgive me.

We were called back into the court. As her hand slipped from mine I tried to preserve in my memory exactly what it felt like to hold Natalie's tiny hand in mine. I resumed my place in the dock, a guard either side of me.

'Mr Cattell,' the judge said, 'please stand.'

I took a big breath and did as I was told. My courage to stand there was in those tablets.

'Guard, please open the dock so Mr Cattell may approach the bench.'

I saw the guards hesitate as they exchanged glances. I looked over at my barrister, but he seemed as confused as I was. I'd been in a crown court enough times to know that the accused only leaves the dock one of two ways: down to the cell or out the door.

I approached the bench until I was within inches of the judge. He had deep creases under his eyes and on his forehead and he smelled like an old musty house. He leaned over his bench and peered down at me.

'Mr Cattell.'

I waited.

'During the fifteen-minute adjournment, something told me that progress can be made in your life, and for that reason, I am going to give you the longest suspended sentence that I possibly can. I'm going to give you five years, suspended for two. I can do that because I'm going to put you in my personal file. I will be keeping an eye on you, Mr Cattell.'

He underlined 'five years' on a piece of paper and waved it in front of me. I stood there, stunned.

I looked up at this decorated man in his long white wig as he started organising the papers on his bench. I knew I was going back to prison. I didn't know what the punch line was, but I stood there waiting for it. He finished putting the papers in his file and looked back down at me.

'Now go out and make progress,' he said and waved me away.

I was more astonished than excited. I'd been granted some more time with my family, but I couldn't celebrate. I still had to be sentenced for the drug charges. The date for that court appearance was four weeks away. I'd met people inside serving five years for exactly the same charges I was facing. If I was found guilty, it was a certain custodial sentence. No matter what miraculous things had been happening in my life, regardless of what Paul thought, I had no choice. I'd have to plead not guilty and hope.

Paul wouldn't let me get away with that decision. He continued to telephone me every other day.

'Please, Steve. You've got to change your plea. You've got to plead guilty.'

'No, Paul. I can't. I've got to fight it. I have to lie my way out of this one, mate. I can't go to prison. I can't do it.'

'You told the truth last time and walked out. Please tell the truth, Steve. Tell the truth and accept Jesus Christ into your life. It's the only way.'

'I can't do that.'

The court was very near where Paul lived. I arrived to find him marching up and down outside the building. His hands were screwed into fists and he was breathing hard.

'I'm telling you Steve, God told me. If you change your plea to guilty, God will set you free.'

'You're talking madness. My barrister reckons I'll be lucky to get four years. If it goes badly today, I could get six.'

'God has told me if you tell the truth today, you will go home tonight.'

Right, I'll go home tonight, I thought. In my wildest dreams I'll go home tonight. There was a wild look in Paul's eyes – I half expected him to get down on his knees to plead with me.

'All right, all right. I'll talk to my barrister. But I'm not going against his advice on this one. There's too much riding on it, mate.'

I went into the court and found my barrister. 'Okay,' I said, 'I know this sounds crazy but I have to ask you a question. Do you think there's any chance I'd get a reduction in sentence if I plead guilty?'

He shook his head. 'It's too late in the day to get any credit for changing your plea to guilty, Steve. If you were to be awarded any kind of reduction at this stage it wouldn't be much.'

'Right. OK. That's what I thought. Thanks,' I said, and I took a little walk down the corridor to think. I'd never even considered my plea before – it never occurred to me not to plead not guilty. But now everything mattered – every day with my family, and every day away from them. Natalie was starting to believe in me again and I knew that as long as I didn't get too much time, she'd stay with me through the sentence. And if it all went wrong, I still had the sleeping tablets. I had nothing to lose.

I walked back to my barrister, who was still sitting on a bench going through his papers. 'I know this won't make sense to you,' I told him, 'but I want to change my plea.'

I was taken into a room with a police officer to write a new statement. This time I didn't have a solicitor: it was just a police officer, a tape recorder and me. I admitted to the charge: intent to supply a class-A drug. That was all I intended to say. I heard a voice continuing on, confessing how long I'd been selling it for and how much money I'd earned. I realised the voice was mine.

'Stop right there, Mr Cattell. If you carry on, you're going to get a longer sentence. I don't want to know all of that. I only want to know about the day you were arrested, OK?'

'It doesn't matter, because I've got to tell you it all. Don't ask me why. That's the way it's got to be.' The urgency in my voice surprised even me.

The police officer just shook his head and sighed.

I felt like I did in that police station when I couldn't stop telling the truth. I heard myself spilling it all and I knew that the longer I talked, the longer I'd get. What was I doing? I should be telling as many lies as possible in order to get a more lenient sentence. I didn't sign the statement until I'd told him everything.

The judge was given a typed version of the statement and I was called back into court. The judge asked the prosecution barrister and my barrister if they had read my new statement.

'I have, your honour.'

'I have, your honour.'

'And prosecution, have you anything to say?'

The prosecution barrister stood and cleared his throat. 'In all the years of prosecuting, your honour, I have never read a more honest and frank statement from a defendant.'

The judge raised his eyebrows. My barrister sat down while the prosecution began to argue the case for my release. There was an extraordinary atmosphere of unreality and disbelief in that courtroom that morning.

I was awarded another suspended sentence.

One Sunday morning I awoke and looked at my beautiful wife curled up next to me. The sun was streaming through the window and, as I had done every day since the court cases several weeks previously, I thought about how lucky I was. I kissed Natalie on the forehead.

'I'm just going to have a bet on the football Nat – I'm feeling lucky!'

I enjoyed the fresh air as I walked down the road to our local betting shop. It was a familiar route, past the bus stop, past the corner shop where I got my cigarettes, past the church. The church. I could hear beautiful music coming from inside. Before I knew what I was doing, I had pushed open the door. About a hundred pairs of eyes turned to look, like when I was arrested at the airport. I quickly slipped into an empty seat at the back.

I prayed – or at least I shut my eyes and said in my head, 'God, I don't know if you're real. I don't know if you exist. But, if you do, thank you for giving me my life back. Thanks for Nat and the children. Thanks for this love, this emotion. Thanks for giving me a new start.'

That done, I decided to leave to place my football bet, but I found that I couldn't. I don't know whether it was embarrassment at everyone turning to look at me that stuck me to my seat or something else. Whatever it was, I sat there for the rest of the service – I couldn't leave God's house. I couldn't even get up to let people beside me out of the pew when the service was over. They had to squeeze past me. After another fifteen minutes passed, the pastor came over to me. He asked me a bit about myself and then prayed for me, and I prayed as well.

Suddenly, like Paul had described to me so many times, I just knew God was real. I felt as though a part of me had always known, but it had only just now fallen into place. I still had loads of questions, and there were so many things I didn't know or understand, but what I did know with absolute certainty was this: there is a God and he is bothered about a man like me. It didn't make any more logical sense than the fact that I got off those certain custodial sentences. God, for reasons known only to himself, loved me and rescued me.

So here I was, Steve Cattell, angry violent crime addict, sitting in God's house and feeling that I belonged there.

13

I went back home what the pastor called a 'born again Christian.' God had forgiven all the terrible things I'd done. God had punished his own Son in my place. The first thing I did as I walked through the door that morning was to pick up my children. Having just experienced the complete, accepting, caring love of my Father God, I understood and felt the relationship between father and child in an entirely new way when I held my kids and heard them call me 'Daddy.' I thought back to that day at the pub when Lillie had lost and found me. Tears sprang to my eyes when I realised that I had also been lost – and found.

I tried to tell Natalie about what had happened, but I don't think I explained it very well. She seemed happy for me, and I knew she was relieved that my life and our relationship was finally beginning to turn around, but I think she was wary, too. I could see it in her eyes. Who could blame her? She'd suffered so much over the years being married to a hardened criminal – and now he was turning into a religious nut.

I couldn't wait to tell Paul. 'You're never going to believe what happened this morning, mate . . .'

I'd never heard him so excited. He cried with me and shared in my joy in such a deep way it was another affirmation of how real God is.

I started attending this Baptist church regularly, although it wasn't always easy. I really liked the pastor, but I struggled to fit in with the other Christians there. They were polite and seemed friendly enough on a Sunday morning, but I noticed that no one invited me for dinner at their home as they did other new members. I'd overhear people making plans to do things together the following week. No one ever asked me. I think the pastor tried to make up for it by inviting me to his house and coming to mine. Sometimes I'd leave a service feeling hurt, rejected, left out. Until I had that experience in the pub garden with Lillie, I'd been immune to all those feelings. I'd been unbreakable, but now I came home from church and cried. I wondered if I should have hidden my life from them – pretended I hadn't been a criminal. Perhaps then they would have wanted to be my friends.

One time when the pastor came to visit me at my house I shared some of my feelings of hurt and rejection.

'You tell me how much God loves me, and I know that's true, and I know that you love and accept me, but you're teaching me how the Bible says that all Christians need to love and encourage each other. Sometimes I can barely face going into that church on a Sunday morning because I know the people there don't want me to be part of anything.'

The pastor had tears in his eyes, too, as he struggled to respond. 'It's not that they don't trust you, Steve – that they think you're going to nick their silver or something – they just haven't met anyone like you before. I think God's using you. I think that's why God's brought you here – so that they can learn.'

Hearing that helped me understand, but I still found it painful. I thought all Christians would accept me just like the pastor did, and it really hurt me when they didn't. Natalie found it hard when I got upset, too. She'd spent years yearning for me to feel emotion and, now that I was, she didn't know how to comfort me. She was still finding my conversion difficult to understand, and my hurt only further alienated her from what she called 'your church.'

I'd been a Christian for about four or five weeks when Paul's girlfriend Maxine phoned to tell me she believed that God wanted me to go to the Care for Ex-Offenders Conference at Holy Trinity Brompton. I had no idea what that was, but she explained it was a conference on Alpha for prisons. I'd heard about Alpha because my pastor had recommended I go on an Alpha course to learn about the basics of the Christian faith. I hadn't gone, and I didn't want to go to the conference either.

Even though people at church didn't let me into their lives, I was already discovering that I led a very different lifestyle from most of them. If I wanted to smoke at this conference, I'd have to hide behind a tree. All the Christians I'd met ate salad and read Christian books. None of them smoked. A full day's conference with Christians would be much harder to handle than a Sunday morning.

Despite my prejudices, Maxine kept encouraging me to go. After what happened in the court and my own experience of God, I took it seriously when Paul and Maxine told me that God had spoken to them. I finally approached my pastor and explained about the conference but told him I couldn't go because I didn't have any money. Four days before the conference, an envelope came through my letterbox. The envelope contained fifty pounds – I was sure it was from the pastor.

I rang the number I'd been given to book my place.

'I'm sorry, Mr Cattell. The conference is fully booked.'

I was about to thank her and hang up. But then I heard myself saying, 'Oh. It's just that a friend of mine has told me that God has spoken to her about me going to this thing.' I went on to explain a bit about myself.

'Just a minute, Mr Cattell.'

I waited on the other end of the phone feeling like a plum. She already told me the conference was fully booked. Why hadn't I let it go at that? Why had I let Maxine talk me into this?

'Mr Cattell?'

'Yes. I'm still here.'

'Sorry about that. Thanks for waiting. If it's God who wants you to come, then you'd better come. We'll see you on Thursday.'

'Oh. OK. That's great. Thank you.'

I said a silent prayer to thank God for providing the money for the conference. But I had this strange sensation. I was certain I felt God telling me I should put the money back in the envelope and put it through the pastor's door. It didn't make sense to me at all. Maybe I wasn't destined to go to this conference, but Maxine had seemed so sure. I decided to do what I thought God had told me and give the money back to my pastor. I put the envelope through his door and then telephoned him to explain why I couldn't accept his kind offer. Then I phoned up another friend and borrowed fifty pounds from him.

On the Thursday morning of the conference I ground my cigarette butt into the ground and crunched up an extra strong mint before I walked up the drive to the church door. The lady sitting behind the desk greeted me with a smile.

'Good morning, Steve.'

I was taken aback. 'Good morning. I don't think we've met. How do you know who I am?'

'I'm the one you spoke with on the phone.'

'How could you know it was me from a phone call?'

'I'm not sure how, I just knew it was you as soon as I saw you. Registration is in the crypt, Steve. Down those stairs.'

There were two hundred and fifty people at that conference, but she knew who I was. God was becoming more and more real, more and more involved in my life – or maybe he always had been, and I was only just starting to realise it.

I went down the stairs to register. There hadn't been much change out of the fifty pounds once I'd bought my train ticket. I stood in the queue behind people handing over their money for the conference. My mouth felt dry. I needed another cigarette. I could see ahead of me that there was a big book on the registration table with all the names of the people attending with the amount of money they still owed next to their names. I hoped I had enough money in my pocket to pay. I was a new Christian and trying to be honest. I didn't want to rip them off.

When I got to the front of the queue I looked down and saw my name at the bottom of the list. It was the only name with four zeros next to it.

'Hello, I'm Steve Cattell,' I said hoarsely. 'How much do I owe?'

He ran his finger down the list to the bottom. 'Nothing, Steve. You're all taken care of. If you go upstairs you can collect your name badge.'

'Thank you.' I hadn't paid anything and I didn't understand, but I didn't have enough money in my pocket to argue so I went upstairs.

Nothing seemed to have started, so I sneaked out for another smoke. There was a little park just to the side of the main door and I hid behind a tree, hoping nobody would see me. I was worried if someone saw me smoking they would think that I wasn't a real Christian and something was wrong with me. I popped another mint in my mouth as I walked around the park and back into the church. As I walked up the drive I passed about forty people outside the main door puffing on their cigarettes. I hadn't realised how tense I was until seeing other Christians smoking made me relax. I went back in smiling to myself.

I milled around a bit. The conference room was upstairs, so I went up and saw a man in the corner with a big sign:

OFFENDERS ANONYMOUS: FREEDOM FROM ADDICTION TO CRIME.

I'd been waiting since I was ten years old to hear those words. I sat down with the man. His name was Joe, and he worked as a councillor for young offenders in Feltham. After seeing the same offenders come back time after time, he'd recognised they had a problem. He felt that they had an addictive lifestyle and that this cycle in their lives needed to be addressed and broken. Their addiction wasn't just to the drink or the drugs, he said, but to the criminal cycle itself. Offenders Anonymous already existed in America and Canada, he told me, but as yet there was nothing in the UK. As he talked about the young offenders he was working with, I knew any of them could have been me thirty years ago. And I knew as I listened to his vision that I passionately wanted to join him – to see Offenders Anonymous set up in this country. I told him the story of my life. He couldn't believe that someone like me, who'd lived the life that I'd lived, was sitting there with him at this conference. We shared the same dream and we agreed to work together to see it realised.

I smiled to myself all the way home on the train that day – because of my excitement about this work with Joe

and because it was the first time I'd agreed to work with
someone to do something legal – without any financial
reward. It felt good. But there was something else to
smile about, too. I saw a glimpse of how God was working in very specific and real ways in my life – through
Maxine, the money from the pastor, the place on the
fully booked conference, the woman who knew me from
the phone call, my meeting with Joe, even through seeing other Christians like me who smoked. I knew this
meeting with Joe was the reason that God wanted me to
be at that conference. On that day, I really started to
believe and trust that God was in control.

I went to church that Sunday after the conference full
of excitement. I wanted to share what I'd learned – my
vision for working with offenders, trying to break their
addiction to crime the way God had broken mine. I
couldn't wait to see huge numbers of people being
brought into the kingdom of God. I thought the whole
church should go out onto the streets and tell criminals,
prostitutes and drug addicts about Jesus. I told people at
the church that the missionary work they'd done over-
seas was good, but no one seemed to be addressing
needs in the community we actually lived in.

One woman folded her arms and I knew she was looking down at me, even though she was a foot shorter.
'You've only been a Christian for six weeks, Steve. You're
on fire now, which is great, but it will die down.'

Despite my frustration with this lady and others like her,
I continued attending my local church and was baptised
– not in a river like Paul, but in a pool inside the church.
The pastor explained the symbolism of baptism, of
dying to your old life and of being cleaned and given a

new life. I was saying goodbye to forty years of crime, forty years of hate and anger. I was excited about this new life, about working with Joe for Offenders Anonymous – I couldn't wait to start working for God.

That night after I was baptised I lay in bed awake. I was certain being baptised was the right thing to do, but my old life still seemed to be holding me back. I tried to pray.

'God, how can I work for you? I've got eighteen months of probation left. Nobody trusts me. I've got no friends. All my old friends from my criminal past have gone. None of the Christians I've met seem to want to know me. I feel so lonely. I feel rejected and unloved.'

I started crying. I'd run out of words, but I knew God understood how I was feeling. For the first time, I heard God speaking to me clearly.

'So was my Son rejected. But you will have every door opened and I will walk beside you every step of the way.'

The first step of this journey for me was, with Joe's encouragement, completing the twelve-step recovery programme of Offenders Anonymous as a 'crime addict.' The programme gave me a way to deal with the addiction that had been the centre of my life for as long as I could remember. I came to appreciate in a new way the miracle that God had accomplished that day in the police station when I told the truth. God had completely freed me from this destructive addiction before I'd even realised I was addicted. Most people in the programme work long and hard to reach that point of freedom. I did have in common with other addicts the difficult balancing act between acknowledging addiction and accepting responsibility. I was sick; I had a problem. But I could not lay those offences at the feet of my addiction and plead insanity. I had to come to terms somehow with the horrendous acts I had committed.

Step Nine, making amends to those people I'd hurt, was really hard. When I thought of the damage I had caused to so many over the years, I was overwhelmed. It wasn't just the victims of my crimes I'd hurt, and there were too many of those to count – but the biggest victims of all had been my family. I hadn't had any idea how much I'd hurt my wife and my children. I completely shut down, trying in vain to block out the memories and feelings. All I could do when I felt like that was pray.

Through all of this I felt the strong and steady hand of my heavenly Father gently guiding me through something that was too big for me to handle on my own. When I began work on this step of the programme, I think part of me was assuming that I might be able to 'make it right.' There were practical steps I could take to make amends. I could show people I'd hurt in the past how much I had changed. I could even pay God back a little by telling these people about him. And in some measure this was all true. But throughout this long and painful process of coming to terms with my past and its consequences, God continually brought me to the incredibly humbling realisation that it wasn't about me. I couldn't do anything in my own strength. When God broke the unbreakable he showed me his glory. I was learning just how powerful God actually is. In my weakness, he is strong.

As I prayed and journeyed through this process of recovery I felt God telling me to go out and help other crime addicts. I wanted to do it, but until I completed the programme and heard God's clear direction I wasn't sure I was ready. The next time I saw my probation officer I told him about it.

'I really think I could help people by going into prisons.'

'Steve, you still have eighteen months of your licence left. You won't be allowed into prisons until that's over. Even then, maybe not for a few years.'

I was gutted.

I started to doubt what God had told me. Paul really seemed to hear clear messages from God, but I didn't find it as easy. Being told I'd have to wait years before I'd be allowed inside a prison didn't exactly feel like a door being opened. I wondered whether I had heard my own voice instead of God's. Maybe I'd taken things back into my own hands again. Was my desire to go into prisons about promoting Offenders Anonymous and me instead of about bringing people to God? The following week Joe gave me letters from seven different US prisoners who had taken part in Offenders Anonymous groups. They'd all gone to the meetings with the intention of changing their criminal lifecycles, but they'd found God. It was all the proof I needed that God was speaking to me and telling me that this was where he wanted me to go.

Everything started to happen quickly. We designed a website for Offenders Anonymous. Paul and I were invited to give our testimonies on Sky's Revelation TV. We went to the television studio and were given about twenty-five minutes each to tell the camera how God had changed our lives. My local paper ran an article on my life and Offenders Anonymous, and then a journalist from *The Times* interviewed me about what I was doing. I knew God was leading me, opening all the right doors at the right time. The more I opened my heart, the more God came in.

It was exciting, but it was a strange time as well. Sometimes I'd be on a real high. My relationships with Natalie and our children had never been as good. I loved them so much – I was only beginning to realise how much I'd changed my life around.

While this change was wonderful, it was on such a massive scale that at times it was difficult to get used to. I'd learned that now that I was a Christian, I belonged to the family of Christ. But before coming to Christ I had belonged to the family of crime – the devil's family. Every friend I'd ever had was a criminal. The people I'd spent my life with stole cars; stabbed people; dealt drugs; burgled houses; robbed banks; they were shoplifters; murderers; fraudsters and worse. But these people accepted me for the person I was. It was painful not finding the same acceptance among the members of God's family. When I'd experienced isolation as a child I'd built up walls to protect myself from hurting. But I didn't want to do that any more. Instead, I clung on to the truth that God had given me – the more I felt rejection, the more I knew Jesus. He'd been rejected like me, but unlike me he didn't deserve it – he'd never done anything wrong.

Paul told me to keep praying. I found the more I prayed and listened to God, the more I trusted what I heard. I prayed a lot about my future with Offenders Anonymous. I would take this journey, God told me, on my own. No one was going to support me – not Christians, not the public, not the government. The only one who would support me in this journey was God, and that would be enough. I thought it very strange when I received this word as a young Christian. I had been taught that when I joined the church I was joined to a family of Christ, and I couldn't believe that nobody there would support what I wanted to do.

The interview that I'd given to *The Times* wasn't published for several months. The day it came out I was at

Faithworks, Steve Chalke's conference in Eastbourne. By
that time I was becoming much more comfortable going
to Christian conferences – probably because I was much
more comfortable with who I was as a Christian in relationship with God. My pastor rang to ask me if I'd seen
the paper. It had been so long since I'd given the interview I'd almost forgotten about it. During a break at the
conference I went out to buy a copy of the paper and
showed the four-page spread to the people who were
with me. Everyone seemed impressed, except me – I
couldn't bring myself to read it. Even in just a few
months, my life had moved on so much that it physic-
ally hurt to face the man I had been, to see it all there in
black and white for the world to read. I hadn't antici-
pated feeling so exposed.

I phoned my pastor back – he'd been so solid ever
since that first day I walked into his church – and tried
to explain how I was feeling.

'I can't read it. Everyone else is reading it and talking
about it and I can't even look at the thing.'

'Look, Steve, talking to me won't help. Go away from
everyone for a bit. Give yourself a bit of space. Go and
sit on a bench near the sea, take your Bible, and pray.'

'What have I done, mate? Why did I give that interview? It's like it will never really be over. I can't face it.'

'I know. It's the most difficult thing in the world to go
back. When you share your life and it's open and you
bare your soul to people, it brings you down.'

'I feel like jumping in the sea and ending it all and I
haven't even read it. I don't know if it's good or bad or
what, but the fact that people I don't know can read
about my whole life and make judgements is terrifying.'

'Of course it is, but Steve, what you've done is really
brave, because not many people would do that. But
what you're doing, showing that crime is an addictive

lifestyle, is important for people to know. Without you people couldn't understand that. You could be saving people you don't even know from spending years and years behind bars. But it will be hard. You are starting on a road that will be terrifying at times, but you have to leave it in God's hands.'

He was absolutely right.

14

Paul and Maxine's wedding was a wonderful celebration and affirmation of God's power to transform lives. God had broken Paul's love for heroin so he was free to love Maxine. I'd been to many weddings, but this was different. It wasn't just a ritual like my weddings had been – a way to get reduced sentences. They were making promises in front of a God I now knew. I thanked God that they had each other and that they had been such a support to me.

At the reception, I met a man called John. He was a schoolteacher and an elder at Paul's church in Northampton. I was a bit wary of him at first because he was so educated. I think I was worried that he'd make fun of me, but I was surprised how interested he was in my life, and especially by the way Paul's conversion had influenced me. After the wedding, John kept in touch with me.

When I first became a Christian, people from the church had told me to be careful, because the devil would want me back. I'd dealt a major blow to his army by leaving it. My house would be attacked, they told me. I hadn't taken it too seriously because, as far as I was concerned, I'd got the manual on the devil. If he came lurking around my house, I was going to beat the crap out of him. That was how I thought you dealt with him. I now believe that the only way you can hurt the devil is by bringing people to know Jesus Christ.

It wasn't long before the attacks that I'd been warned about began. Life at home became almost unbearable. I found it hard to provide for my family financially. All I was trained to do was to break into houses and obtain money by illegal means. I was trying to support my wife and three children with no qualifications and very little work experience. My eight-year-old daughter started having terrible nightmares. My house was in turmoil. I had no idea what to do. Natalie and I went for a walk one evening to talk it through and as I stood on a bridge holding her hand and staring down at the water, all I wanted to do was jump.

I found it hard to accept – I was a changed man. But my family was taking an awful beating. Where was the family in Christ? My church 'family' had warned me this would happen, but then they left me alone to deal with it myself. I still wanted desperately to fit in with other Christians. I had a different background from the people at church, but my future was the same. I constantly found myself struggling with whether the rejection from the church reflected God's rejection of me. Was God trying to tell me something through all these godly people, who had known God a lot longer than I had, wanting nothing to do with me?

The pastor had asked two men at the church to mentor me through the early stages of my Christian life. Although they tried, I was sure they were only doing it because they'd been asked – not because they wanted to. I'd always resented people helping me out of duty or pity. Becoming a Christian hadn't changed that. So I withdrew.

John, who I'd met at Paul's wedding, was the only one who supported me through this time. He rang me up regularly and he listened to me. He seemed to care about my life and about the struggles I was having. He prayed with me over the phone. That was the extent of my Christian fellowship.

When I did my testimony on Revelation TV with Paul, I sent a copy of it, on DVD, to every prison in the country. Prison chaplaincies get sent all sorts of material, so I wasn't expecting a massive response – many chaplains wouldn't have watched it. Only two prisons got back to me within six months and invited me to visit. I don't know whether it was God's sense of humour, or maybe he was laying those demons to rest, but the first prison to contact me was Camp Hill, the place on Isle of Wight where I had spent eighteen months in solitary confinement, where I had screamed and prayed for the devil.

I had never visited a prison except as an inmate. I didn't know what to expect. As I stood on the deck of the ferry, I wondered how seeing it would make me feel. I wondered what the chaplain would be like. I assumed he'd meet me at the gate, maybe have a chat with me and a cup of tea. Instead, as soon as I arrived, he took me on a guided tour that began in the punishment block. It was strange – the chaplain had known nothing about the eighteen months I spent there. I looked inside a cell and felt amazement that I had lived there in that tiny space for so long. It was a warm day, but the punishment block was cold – very cold and very dark and very evil. There was a sense of something there. The chaplain didn't seem feel it, but I did.

After my tour, the chaplain asked if I would take part in the service later. I was surprised, because I'd never been asked to help in a service at my church. I was a lowly Christian who'd really sinned – not one of those educated Christians who knew the Bible off by heart and only needed to be forgiven for swearing a few times. I had never done anything besides sit at the back of the church and listen. I enjoyed taking part in the service at the prison, but my reaction to his request helped me to see more clearly the extent of the betrayal I felt by my church family.

The second prison that invited me to visit was Rochester. Its name had changed, but it was the borstal where I'd hit the governor on the head with a stool and did six months isolation in total silence.

Once again, I arrived after a long journey and the chaplain marched me straight down to the punishment block to begin my guided tour. It hadn't changed very much.

There were two seventeen-year-old boys in the block. The chaplain, who was a woman, asked the prison officers if I could speak with them. They agreed. I explained to the boys who I was and told them a little bit about myself. I also told them about Offenders Anonymous. We talked for a few minutes about what they'd done and why they were there. They didn't say much to start with, but when I told them about my life as a burglar they seemed more interested.

'I love doing burglaries,' one of them told me.

'Love?' I said. 'Love itself is healthy, but loving to burgle people's homes is an unhealthy addiction. If you can sit in this punishment block in the middle of a sentence at seventeen years of age and admit to loving burglaries, you will not be able to escape that lifestyle. As soon as you're released, you'll do it again.'

The boy nodded.

The other one clenched his fist so the knuckles went white. 'But Steve, when you get through that front door and no one's there, and when you find the jewellery box . . .

'You're getting an adrenaline rush just thinking about burgling – that's what I'm talking about. It's not healthy. It will destroy you,' I told him.

'But that feeling?'

'I know that feeling. I used to get it – just the same as you. But I've escaped. I get that feeling now when Arsenal win – when they score a goal in the final minutes. That's a healthy rush of adrenaline. But if you get that feeling thinking about burgling someone's home, what do you think you'll do when you get out?'

The boys looked at each other. 'Yeah, I suppose we are addicted to it,' one of them admitted.

At that moment I knew I had to get into every prison in the country. The chaplain was amazed by how quickly those boys had opened up to me. She approached the governor about me coming to the prison in a more official capacity to work with the young offenders.

He refused. 'We don't have ex-cons.'

Being in those punishment blocks brought back a lot of memories. I'd spent the past year trying to forget how it felt to be locked in isolation – the lonely days, the long nights, the endless abuse, the silence, the letters that came, the relationships that broke up – I found myself reliving it all.

But these memories helped me to understand that everything I'd experienced, I'd experienced for a reason. Despite what my probation officer had said about me not being allowed into prisons while still under my licence, I had been to two. So I knew I couldn't give up. I could trust God to open the doors for me where they should have been closed.

I still hadn't been invited round for a coffee or a meal by anyone from church. Each Sunday I forced myself to go to the service. I reminded myself that I'd been forgiven for my past and I had every right to worship God, along with everyone else there.

I invited a Christian friend called Ray to go with me one week. After the service, we sat down in the foyer and watched people leave.

'It's strange,' he said. 'Everybody's walked past and said "Hello" and wanted to talk to me, but nobody seems interested in you. Yet God's been doing so much work in your life. The fact that they haven't wanted to share in those experiences amazes me. I'd have thought they'd want you up at the front.'

'Yeah, well, they only want people from Bible college to stand in front of the church. They want someone who's come from a mission in Africa. They want people of standing in the church – of standing in the community. They want people who run the Bible class for the youth, the people who run the Alpha groups. They want the established members of the church to talk to the church. If I was invited to speak on a Sunday, I would stand up and talk about the realities of where we live today. I would open the eyes of the congregation in a different way. They would want to talk about God in their middle-class world. But I wouldn't say what they want to hear.'

I knew that if God wanted me to reach people, it wasn't going to be through the church. That door had closed.

I really wanted Natalie to share my faith in God. I prayed for her, but I didn't want to force her. I'd forced and manipulated her too much in the past. She was interested in this new part of my life, but she found it hard when I came home from church feeling depressed. I'm sure she wondered why I still went.

But she, more than anyone, could see the massive change in me. She knew only a miracle could have changed me that much. I was a different man. She had spent her life trying to make me a better husband, a better father, a better person. But only God could do that. In time God worked in her heart to reveal his power and love to her and she became a Christian too.

Our shared faith continued to make us stronger. I knew I was blessed to have her in my life, and I knew that I'd given her countless reasons to leave me. Many people had asked her why she'd stayed, and she always said that she believed relationships needed to be worked at – that no marriage is ever over – you have to fight and fight to make it work. I didn't deserve her and I thanked God that he'd put her in my life and given her the strength and patience to fight through all those years.

Natalie supported what I felt God wanted me to do and she encouraged me to keep trying to get into prisons. She also helped me through all of my growth and recovery to see that it wasn't all about me – that the families of crime addicts were their biggest victims.

Out of the blue one day I had a phone call from a college catering for inner-city students in Hertfordshire. They asked if I'd be willing to come into a class and talk to the youth about the dangers of crime and drugs. I wasn't sure whether to accept the invitation or not. I wanted to go into prisons – a school was something completely different.

Natalie persuaded me to go.

'I think you have to be open to God having plans for you that you haven't thought about, Steve. That's what you keep telling me about God,' she smiled. 'How he's so much bigger and far beyond what we can imagine ourselves.'

I smiled back and nodded. 'OK. You have me there.'

'So even though you haven't knocked on this particular door, God might be opening it. Do you remember telling me about how when you stole from the sweet shop as a kid you had no idea you'd be drawn into the cycle of crime? Maybe God's saying you can help people at a different stage of the cycle – maybe even before it begins. Some of the kids at this college might be going down the same road you were.'

'You're right,' I said. 'But you'll have to pray for me. Hard.'

'I will,' she laughed.

I realised that, with all of my painful memories of prison, it was still an environment where I felt within my comfort zone. I knew criminals – the way they thought, how they operated. And I'd survived inside. School was another matter. They wouldn't let me out of prison, but most of the time I was supposed to be in school they wouldn't let me in.

I was terrified walking into that classroom. Kids were whispering, shouting, throwing things. I wanted to run away. I hadn't really prepared anything as I hadn't been at all sure what it would be like. I began by introducing myself. As I was telling them I'd been in prison for twenty-four years, the door burst open. A boy sauntered in – I thought it was a boy, although he had his hood pulled right over his head so I couldn't see his face.

He laughed at me. 'All we want to know about prison is whether it's true what they say about what happens in the showers.'

The class started sniggering.

I walked over to him, bent down and peered under his hood. 'Nah,' I said, 'With a face like yours, you've no need to worry.'

The class sniggered again, but now I had their attention. The boy who'd made the comment sat down at his desk. The class listened while I explained that taking cocaine increases your heart rate so much that your body can't function properly. I told them about the withdrawal pains from heroin and how many people I'd known who were now dead from it. I told them about crime – how hard it was for me to break the cycle. They listened quietly for the whole lesson.

When the bell rang they went outside for a cigarette. I joined them. Some kids told me it was the best lesson they'd ever had and asked me if I was coming back next week. One of them admitted she was on bail for burglary. Another one had been cautioned for shoplifting. The school didn't even know.

Six different teachers had come in during my talk to listen. Before I left, they asked me if I was available to give talks to their classes. I talked to two classes every day for two weeks. I met one of the students in a shop on Christmas Eve. He told me that he'd been at one of my talks and that I'd helped him realise how addictive the criminal lifestyle could be. He told me that when he left college he was going to get a job. When he had a family he was going to love them and bring his children up to be honest.

I began to get offers from other schools and colleges, and soon I was giving talks several times a week. It was, as Natalie said, another door that God had opened.

But God still reminded me of the truth of suffering and rejection from time to time. The day before I was booked to give a talk in one college that I hadn't been to before, I had a phone call from the college secretary. She explained that the head of the college didn't deem it appropriate for a former criminal to come in and talk to the students. It hit me hard. I put the phone down and kicked one of Lillie's toys across the room. It clattered into the wall and Natalie rushed in.

'That's it!' I shouted. 'Stuff them all. I'm not going to bother with this any more.'

'What's wrong?'

'They don't want me. They don't think I'm appropriate! I'll give them appropriate . . .' I seethed. 'Like those

kids are immune to the real world. That's inappropri-
ate!'

'Steve, it's not you they don't want. That's the devil.
That's the devil trying to bring you down and destroy
everything that God wants you to do. Now you pick
yourself up and you carry on, because you know what
you're doing is right.'

I went into our bedroom and shut the door. I was gutted. I didn't even feel like praying. Then I remembered
what God had told me, 'So was my Son rejected. But you
will have every door opened and I will walk beside you
every step of the way.'

I decided that Natalie was right. I was not going to be
beaten. God had given me a job to do. I worked for God.
God employed me. I had to take the ups and I had to
take the downs. I pulled myself up, found Natalie in the
kitchen, and hugged her.

I visited a comprehensive school later that week to
give a talk in an A-level Psychology class. I gave my talk
as usual and, although it went fairly well, I came away
still feeling low about the college that didn't want me. I
drove straight to my next class at another college, where
I gave an hour's talk and then asked if there were any
questions. The door opened and a man I didn't recog-
nise came in and told me there was a car waiting for me.
There was another college that I needed to talk to.

'Hang on. I haven't even finished this one yet,' I told
him. I hadn't booked another class that day.

'But they're waiting for you,' he said.

As we walked to his car, he told me that we were
going to the college that had rung to cancel me. Two
hundred students had overruled the head of this college
– they wanted me to come. I assumed I would be taking
a class, but instead I found myself speaking to a hundred and fifty students.

I still find talking in schools and colleges strange. I'm not academically gifted and it's not where I'm comfortable. But God has brought me here and when I sit and relate my past, and all the dangers of this world, and the trauma and the pain of the victims, and the addictions, and everything else, I know it's what I should be doing. I know this when I finish a lecture and, instead of going off for their break – their cigarette or their lunch – the kids crowd around me. They ask me questions, shake my hand and tell me it was the best lecture they've ever had. This is where God wants me.

God 1 – Devil 0.

The devil didn't beat me. I'm still here, and I'm still fighting. I will be rejected. People will think I'm scum of the earth. But I'll stand up and I'll walk through that, because God is with me.

Could I have opened those doors myself? An ex-con with a bad life and a bad history? No way. God opened those doors. All I have to do is keep walking through them and delivering the message. It's not easy. I find it difficult to get on with people outside the criminal world and to communicate. I know how to talk about heroin – how much it weighs and how much it sells for and what it does to you. But I don't know how to talk about everyday life. It's all new.

15

I'm never going to escape my past. Even though my past is gone – it's over – I'm never going to be able to forget. No matter where I go, or what I do, my past is always going to be a part of my present. The big difference is that it doesn't bring me down because I've been for-given and God is showing me how to use my past in a positive way. I've done so many bad things in my life, but I've repented and I've been forgiven because of the price Jesus paid for me on the cross. God has given me new life in him, and I'm doing my best to use this sec-ond chance to bring glory to him. The fear in my victims' eyes, the traumas, everything that I've done all my life – I've been there and I'm passionate that this generation, this culture, understand the dangers of that sort of life. So I'm still fighting, but this is a fight with a purpose and I'm not out for my reputation – it's God's reputation I care about.

Part of my battle is with a past that pulls me still. The criminal life isn't glamorous; it's very painful. But it's exciting – a continual adrenaline rush.

It's midnight and I'm in bed. All of a sudden there's a knock at the door. Instantly I'm out of bed, pulling on a pair of jeans. I open the back window, ready to run. It sounds like the police. Bang, bang, bang. That's the knock of a policeman. I'm out the back window and jumping over fences. I've got no shoes on, no socks. It's freezing cold. I'm seven gardens down, hiding behind someone's shed. I've got stones in my feet and I can hear my heart pumping. Then I hear my wife shouting out, 'It's no one, just someone for next door. They just got the wrong house.'

Every time a car pulls up, I get up, looking out of the window, ready to jump out and run.

I'm driving. A car pulls out behind me, so I do a left and another left, a circle. Just to make sure I'm not being followed. Just to make sure the police aren't on to me.

People will grass on you if they get arrested. They'll grass to get bail. They'll grass to get a lighter sentence. You're never safe.

You can't tell people where you're living. You can't tell your friends your address. You're always watching, always looking over your shoulder, always waiting.

The pace of that life was extreme, and sometimes I do miss it. More than once since I became a Christian I've gone upstairs to my wardrobe and started throwing all my clothes in a case.

'That's it! I've had enough. I'm going.'

It's not that I don't love my wife and children – I do. It's just that the life I lived for more than thirty-three years was exhilarating, and sometimes it tries to pull me back. I used to despise people with nine to five jobs. I used to mock them and rob them. Now I'm trying my best to be one of them. Going straight, earning money the hard way; paying bills – it's hard, and it can be boring. But then, if the temptation weren't there, we wouldn't have a devil. He wouldn't exist. And every time I resist I know God is making me stronger, more like Jesus.

One advantage of having lived in the criminal world is that I know the devil is real. I know he will try to pull me down. I know I've got to fight him. Now that I've left that life, he comes after me more. He's not so bothered with the ones out there who haven't given their lives to Jesus. They're already part of his team, whether they believe in him or not. But I've left his world and his lies. So I'm constantly fighting the temptation and the attacks. Although I've packed my case more than once, I've never actually left. God has held on to me. But there are still times, when depression comes thick and I get so bogged down in all the terrible things in my past, that I lose sight of God's love and his acceptance.

In those times, I have to cling on to the truth – Jesus took my crimes upon himself when he died on the cross. He set me free from my past so that I could have a future.

I went back to St Paul's Church one day – that empty church where I first asked God to help me. I went on a Wednesday, the same time of day I went all those months ago, but when I tried the door it was locked. I tried the following week and the week after that, but I never found it open.

I returned one Sunday and spoke to the pastor after the service. I explained my story and asked him why the church had been open on that particular day at that particular time. His old grey eyes sparkled with life.

He looked directly into my eyes. "I think you know why,' he said. And he was right. I think God slipped back the lock at 12:45 on that Wednesday. I think he was expecting me. And he has a plan for me.

I'm still learning. When I found out my parents weren't my real parents, I lost the will to trust people. I didn't believe in anyone. I relied on myself and trusted no one. I'm slowly learning to trust people again. I'm learning to trust God. I'm beginning to have confidence that God knows what's best for me and allows things to happen for a reason. He made sure I didn't go into a

prison until he knew I could face going into a punishment block. He didn't allow me back into the darkness
until he knew I could find my way back to the light.

All I ask for people to do is to support me in prayer –
so that I can use my experience of darkness to help save
some of those who are caught up in its cycle. Life is
about the doors that God opens: the prison that I'm not
supposed to be allowed to go into, colleges and schools,
housing estates and churches, conferences. The devil
continues to lure me into depression and to bring up my
past to haunt me. He will always try to put barriers in
my way to try to stop me from doing the work that God
has given me. There are times when I want to stop, sit
back in my armchair, relax, and enjoy my caravan and
my children. But I know that would be wrong, because
that would be allowing the devil a foothold.

My house today is a loving home. My children are
now growing up in a more normal family, and I'm there
to see them. I no longer leave the house wondering if the
next time I see them will be in a prison visitors' lounge.
I can't get back the years I lost, but I'm thankful I have
this chance to try to make up for them.

I stayed at the Baptist church for two years and during that time things did get better. I understand now that
I was part of the problem. I had to learn how to sit over
a cup of tea with people from a world I had never lived
in. In some ways I'm grateful for the experience I had
there – if I'd had more support humanly speaking, I'd
never have learned to rely on God the way that I do now.
I've since started attending Hatfield Elim Church. The
pastor and his wife have a vision, which I share, to reach
the local youth on the streets – and I know I can be of
help in making that vision a reality. I still can't sit after
church talking about the weather or the garden – I am
always talking about those who are trapped in a world

of drugs or crime. If people aren't willing to talk about that, then they will talk to someone else after church – and that's OK.

I have had to learn patience, to accept that I can't force my way into prisons, churches and colleges. Before I became a Christian, I got what I wanted by holding a gun to someone's head. Now if I want something I have to pray and ask God. He's my Dad. He'll either give me it or he won't. That's the kind of relationship I've got with him. And he has given me a lot.

Offenders Anonymous groups now meet in many prisons across the country. Every week I receive invitations to talk in schools, prisons and, yes, even churches. Last year I was one of the speakers at a conference at the Birmingham NEC. The panel was mostly made up of policemen – I was the only ex-offender. I spoke to seven thousand people about addressing crime addiction.

Whatever it was in that police station that made me tell the truth still controls my tongue. Wherever I go, I'm open and honest about my past. It's not hidden from God, so why should I hide it from anyone else? Every house on my street now has a burglar alarm!

If I hadn't cried out for God, if I hadn't allowed him to come in and turn my life around, I know exactly how it would have ended. One day I'd have been an old and lonely man – with no family, no friends, no one bothering about me. They'd have taken me out from a prison cell in a body bag. Stan died alone. No one came to his funeral. Countless people I knew – people whose names I don't even remember – hanged themselves, slashed their wrists, overdosed, and I was heading the same way. I didn't know how to stop and change direction. Maybe sometimes I didn't even want to change, but I know that often in the darker times I did – I just couldn't do it on my own.

Because of God, and only because of him, I'm living surrounded by my loved ones – my wife, my children, my grandchildren. And when I die, having lived a life of loving and being loved, it will be only the beginning in the kingdom of heaven.

I'm learning that nothing is impossible for God. No one is outside his forgiveness – all anyone has to do is ask. And if God is there for a man like me, breaking the unbreakable and mending the broken heart of a broken man, he's there for everyone.